Fixation to Freedom
The Enneagram of Liberation
Eli Jaxon-Bear

Also by Eli Jaxon-Bear

*An Outlaw Makes It Home: The Awakening
of a Spiritual Revolutionary* (2018)

Wake Up and Roar: Satsang with Papaji (1992, 2016)

*Sudden Awakening: Stop Your Mind, Open Your Heart,
and Discover Your True Nature* (2001, 2015)

Lied der Freiheit (1998)

Cosmic Jokes and Teaching Stories (1990)

*Healing the Heart of Suffering: Using the Enneagram
for Spiritual Growth* (1989)

Fixation to Freedom

The Enneagram of Liberation

Eli Jaxon-Bear

Fixation to Freedom: The Enneagram of Liberation
2006 by Eli Jaxon-Bear

Fourth Printing 2019

New Morning Books
Ashland, OR U.S.A.
(541) 201-0900
www.newmorningbooks.com

Interior Design: Patt Narrowe
Cover Design: tatlin.net
Editing Assistance: Margi Wainio, Jared Franks and Leigh Estok
Printed in the United States of America

ISBN: 978-1-7329523-4-8

Library of Congress Catalog Card 2019937253

Your true nature is happiness and bliss.

– Sri Ramana Maharshi
(30 December 1879 – 14 April 1950)

TABLE OF CONTENTS

Your true nature is happiness and bliss.

– Sri Ramana Maharshi
(30 December 1879 – 14 April 1950)

PART I

GATEWAY TO FREEDOM: THE NATURE OF REALITY

The Desire for Happiness

Everyone wants to be happy. This is a universal component of the human condition and may seem so self-evident that it does not bear noting. Even those who hate themselves intensely or do violence to others can trace the drive back to the deepest unfulfilled desire for happiness.

Why is it that so few are truly happy? If it is true that our nature is happiness and bliss, why has it been so rare for people to realize this about themselves and to live their lives in gratitude and love?

How is it that the universal quest for happiness has led to the full spectrum of suffering on this planet? Even the most extreme expressions of war, murder, rape, and environmental devastation can all ultimately be traced back to the human desire for happiness.

How can the desire for happiness manifest as ignorance, greed, and violence? The Enneagram offers an answer to this puzzle and points to the solution.

• • •

This inconceivable gateway of great liberation is in everyone.
It has never been blocked; it has never been defective. Buddhas
and Chan Masters have appeared in the world and provided
expedient methods, with many different devices, using illusory
medicine to cure illusory disease.

– Chan Master Yuansou

Passing through the gateway of liberation is the entrance to happiness, bliss, and the knowledge of one's true identity. In the past, it has been the rarest of events. When a great soul passes through to liberation, like the Buddha, it is an event of such magnitude that it is remembered for thousands of years. Yet, these great beings then become objects of worship, as if it were something that happened to someone else a long time ago and does not relate to our present situation except as an object of prayer.

This gateway of liberation is in everyone. It is the fulfillment of our human potential to pass through the gateway. The human species is still evolving. It is a race against time. Will we evolve to the next stage of our potential unfolding or will we destroy the Earth's ability to sustain us before we get there?

The ones who have awakened to their true nature as happiness and bliss were the forerunners, the harbingers of things to come. Now it is possible, not just for a few great souls but for everyone to awaken to his or her true nature. The seeds are being cast to the winds. The great gateway of liberation is open, and all may pass through.

In our time, the Enneagram has appeared as an illusory medicine to cure an illusory disease. The disease is the egoic idea of separation. The cure is to look in the wisdom mirror of the Enneagram to see past all false identification to the truth of being.

•   •   •

Roots of The Sacred Enneagram

This teaching originated around two thousand six hundred years ago with the pre-Socratic Greek philosopher Pythagoras. Pythagoras was the first person to call the universe, "the cosmos,"[1] thereby, in one revolutionary stroke, putting the universe at the center of everything, instead of man or earth. Cosmos means two things in Greek: Interconnected and Harmonious. Pythagoras, called the first mathematician by Aristotle, developed the Enneagram, based on triangles and octaves, as a way to express mathematically the harmony of the cosmos. The Pythagorean Theorem is an example of his interest in the inner mathematics of geometry. The first drawing of the Enneagram comes from one of Pythagoras' students and is an expression of the mathematics and harmonics of materialization.[2] By applying this model to the human psyche, the nature of the human mind is given a concrete form and true character and essence can be discerned and expressed.

According to Wikipedia, "Plato may have borrowed from Pythagoras the idea that mathematics and abstract thought are a secure basis for philosophy, science, and morality. Plato and Pythagoras shared a 'mystical approach to the soul and its place in the material world.'" Pythagoras believed that souls reincarnate and that he could remember several of his past lives. He said we have direct knowledge, or gnosis, by recalling what we already

---

[1] Kosmos in Greek; Philosophy Before Socrates, Richard D McKirahan (Hackette Publishing) page 92.

[2] Pythagoras left no writing behind. Everything we know about his teaching comes from either his students or contemporary reports. See the Enneagram drawn in Pythagoras, Thomas Stanley (Ibis Press) page 166.

know when the mind is empty so that the depth of wisdom can reveal itself.

Starting with Pythagoras' first mystery brotherhood in Ancient Greece, the teaching has mostly been kept secret to this day. We can assume that at some point this community of initiates, who held all material things in common as well as passing on the sacred teaching for those souls ripe enough to receive it, crossed the border to the Persian empire.[3] To survive in hostile religious societies, the teachings went underground. The sacred was hidden from the profane, and the mystery schools and brotherhoods passed on their teaching from generation to generation.

In our age, the Enneagram first came to light in the west in the teachings of G. I. Gurdjieff, who was a mystic, philosopher, spiritual teacher, and composer of Armenian and Greek descent, born in Armenia in the late nineteenth century.[4] Gurdjieff claimed to have learned his teaching from a mystery school in Central Asia.

The Enneagram next appeared in the west through Oscar Ichazo, a teacher in Arica, Chile, who started his spiritual school, The Arica Institute, which taught his version of the Enneagram. Ichazo took the teaching out of the abstract and developed the characteristics of nine different fixations with easily recognizable features. This was revolutionary. However, because he called it The Enneagram of Personality, it limited the depth of the inquiry to superficial changes of personality or to working on perfecting a better fixation.

---

[3] While conjecture on my part, it is based on the historical record of the Roman Emperor Justinian's shutting down the last of Plato's philosophy academies in Athens, and the teaching staff entering into the Persian empire. Also note that by the time of the Zhou Dynasty in China, which ended in 256BC, there was a written proof of the Pythagorean theorem, showing how far the teaching had spread. See The Lives of the Eminent Philosophers, translation of Diogenese Laertius by Pamela Mensch, Oxford University Press, page 400.
[4] *In Search of the Miraculous*, P.D. Ouspenksy. A full explanation of Gurdjieff's teaching by one of his students. Note the relationship between Gurdjieff's cosmology and the Druze in Russell's book mentioned on the next pages. Clearly Gurdjieff's metaphysics is the same as Pythagarus'.

Claudio Naranjo, a psychotherapist and a student of Ichazo, took the teaching to Berkeley, California where it was fleshed out with psychological depth. Gurdjieff never went further in his public analysis than to say that each fixation and every person has a chief feature. He claimed that the deluded Russians he was working with in his school would literally die of shock if they were to ever know their chief feature.

By the 1980s, I had learned this system from Jerry Perkins, his teacher Kathleen Speeth, and her teacher Claudio Naranjo. While each gave me an important perspective and many insights, they were teaching it as a personality system. I found that view limiting and while developing my own perspective and teaching, I searched for the source.

After many years of research, traveling, and searching I have discovered that this Pythagorean teaching is still alive and hidden, in at least one place -- the Druze of Lebanon. In his amazing book, Heirs to Forgotten Kingdoms, Gerard Russell, a former British diplomat in the Middle East, set out to find the last of the pre-Islamic religions. He finds a remarkable number and along the way discovers the Druze and their connection to Pythagoras. In an interview with a Druze University professor, he asked if the Druze were successors to the Pythagoreans. The professor deflects from a direct answer and says, "To reveal a truth to man unready to accept it is three sins at once. It makes him disbelieve the truth, makes him think wrongly about you, and makes him say, 'the truth is nonsense.' "[5]

In our time, secret teachings are being made public and the sacred is being brought into the everyday world. Often the teachings become watered down and commercialized for mass appeal. This has been the fate of the Enneagram of personality, which even when "spiritualized" in the nineties, still assumes a fixated someone who becomes more spiritual with practice.

---

[5] *Heirs to Forgotten Kingdoms*, Gerard Russell (Simon and Schuster) p.172.

Fortunately, I never took the vows of secrecy. Those vows come after years of being tested in silence, as required by Pythagoras and his descendants. We now call it the Enneagram of Liberation. It is a sacred, previously secret teaching. Pythagoras believed it took many lifetimes of learning and purification before a soul was ready to receive the secret. My teacher said, "If you made it this far, you are ready to go all the way."

A Vehicle for Self-Inquiry

The personal entity, which identifies its existence with life in the physical body and calls itself "I," is the ego.

The physical body, which is inherently inert, has no ego sense.

The Self, which is pure consciousness, has no ego sense.

Between these two, there mysteriously arises the ego sense, which is the "I" thought.

This ego, or separate personal identity, is at the root of all suffering in life. Therefore, it is to be destroyed by any means possible. This is Liberation or Enlightenment or Self-realization.

– Ramana Maharshi

There is a living intelligence in all people that seeks ultimately to discover its source and true identity. The teaching of Ramana Maharshi is to plunge inside to discover who you really are, and realize yourself as the true self, not the ego. While universally recognized as an enlightened saint, he was not the first to inquire into himself.

Know Yourself was inscribed on the entrance to an Apollonian temple in Athens well before Socrates said, "An unexamined life is not worth living." In the ancient Greek of Herodotus, the first historian, history and inquiry were the same word: the act of seeking knowledge. This is the frame of mind that leads to self-knowledge and has birthed traditions of awakening around the world.

The method of self-inquiry my teacher, a devotee of Ramana Maharshi, taught me, is to silence the mind and look within to find out what the *I* is made of. This inquiry can start by seeing what you have falsely identified as yourself. The Enneagram, as presented here, is an invaluable aid in inquiry into your true nature by first clearly showing who you are not. When all your thoughts, mental stories, emotions, and body sensations are directly investigated, they are seen to not be who you are. They are all ever-changing and mechanical, while you are what does not disappear or change. You can directly realize that you are the consciousness that gives rise to all perception and experience.

When the realization of oneself as pure consciousness is learned, or studied, or believed, it becomes a mental concept. This is the mind's idea instead of direct reality. Pythagoras might say that this conceptualization of truth is the result of giving the truth to those not prepared to receive it.

Realization must be directly experienced and intelligently investigated to discover it for yourself. In the plunge within, the *I* that is plunging, the same *I* that is reading this page, is discovered to be merely an idea.

It is a fortunate and mysterious moment when the desire for happiness leads to the consideration of whether this that has been called *me* is real. In the light of self-inquiry, limitations that once seemed to define oneself are discovered to be more like transparent lines drawn on water. They exist only on the surface of conscious-ness in one's imagination. When these illusions of mind are clearly exposed, true limitless being reveals itself.

In service of this ultimate discovery, the Enneagram appears as a wisdom mirror for consciousness to recognize how it has become falsely identified with particular forms. In its subtle depth, the Enneagram reveals patterns of subconscious physical, mental, and emotional identification. The core identification is the thought, "I am somebody." Once this thought arises, the ego becomes crystal-lized in the mind, and consciousness experiences itself as limited.

Pythagoras taught that the first dichotomy is between limited and limitless. In my experience, the first limitation is the sense that who one is, is inside, and who one is not, is outside. "*I*" now has a narrow identity as an object in space that is called *me* or *myself*. The Enneagram clearly describes the nine variations of this basic belief that one is a limited and separate body.

My teacher told us about waves. The waves are continually racing toward the shore where they roll, crash, and then slide back to regroup, and roll and crash again. Each wave has its own unique moment and movement, its own size and roll, and seems different from all other waves.

One day a little wave became curious as it saw a big, old wave coming from far away. The little wave approached the big wave and said, "You seem like a big, old, wise wave. You have traveled so far and seen so much. Maybe you can tell me, is there such a thing as an ocean?"

The old wave smiled and said, "Well, I have heard of the ocean, but I haven't actually seen it."

With the Enneagram you can discover how you have believed yourself to be a wave, separate from the ocean of consciousness. Once you have clearly recognized the structure of mind, you then have a choice. You can either continue to believe yourself to be a limited "me," or you can begin to fully examine the false belief that who you are is bound by time and form. In order to choose the latter, a desire must arise within the ego for the transcendence of ego. There must arise a burning desire for freedom, truth, or God.

With conscious surrender of limited identification comes a great relaxation. There is an unwillingness to continue playing a self-destructive mental game. When the game of suffering stops, there is vast realization. What is discovered to be underneath all identification is the ocean of supreme bliss and peace. This is the beginning.

Using the Enneagram

My Child, Because you think you are the body, for a long time you have been bound. Know you are pure awareness. With this knowledge as your sword, cut through your chains and be happy!

– Ashtavakra Gita

The great gift of the Enneagram of Character Fixation is that it gives us the precise structure of the knot of ego. Awareness is our sword, and the Enneagram shows us the knot that needs to be cut. In this way enlightenment, or self-realization, is possible.

The Enneagram reveals how we have falsely identified "I" as the physical, emotional, and mental bodies. This identification presents itself in the unexamined belief that we are a body with behaviors, feelings, and thoughts. Once these patterns of subconscious identification are brought to light, they can be discarded in the search for the true "I." In this way, the Enneagram is immediately useful in the process of awakening, or enlightenment.

There is a well-known Sufi story about Mullah Nasr Id'n, out at night under a street lamp on his hands and knees, frantically searching.

A friend comes along and asks, "What are you doing?" The Mullah replies, "I am searching for my keys." His friend asks, "You lost them under the light?" The Mullah looks up, grinning, and replies, "No, actually, I lost them over in those dark bushes by the door, but the light here is so much better for seeing."

When we look under the streetlight for what we know is lying in the shadows, we console ourselves with the activity of the search and eventually feel frustrated when what we find does not prove to be lasting. When we are ready to look directly at that which we have masked and justified, the Enneagram gives us light—reflecting light without judgment. It provides us the opportunity to see the mechanical nature of the ego that we have identified as "self." In this way, the Enneagram is extremely precise in its description of what is false, so that what is true may be revealed.

As I mentioned earlier, George Gurdjieff, one of the first spiritual teachers in the West to use the Enneagram system with his students, said that everyone has what he called a "chief feature." This chief feature is the part of our egoic identity that is the hardest for us to see, like seeing the tip of our nose without a mirror. The overall pattern of our thoughts, feelings, and behaviors seems so real and so personal to us that we have incorrectly identified it to be who we are. It is the pervasive background quality of this chief feature that keeps it from being directly examined. In fact, this feature is both the obstruction and the potential gateway to realizing who we really are.

Gurdjieff based his work on creating conscious shocks for the awakening of consciousness to self-awareness. The Enneagram is that shock.

Like any powerful medicine, the Enneagram can also very easily be misused. The danger is in recognizing the patterns of identification, and then using this insight to justify their continuation. For example, "Oh, well, since I'm a Five, I have to retreat." Or, "I'm an Eight, so I'm just being myself when I get in a rage." I see this kind of justification often. Or it is used to frame another in a box by saying, "Oh, that is just your fixation." This is the danger. Rather than a pure, reflective mirror, the sacred Enneagram then becomes just another way to maintain the ego sense rather than facing the ego and seeing through it.

When treated casually, everything holy turns to poison. Just as sacramental wine misused leads to drunken stupor, all truth that is treated casually leads to belief systems that foster spiritual ego. If you treat the Enneagram with respect, it is a great medicine. Treat it casually, and it is a great poison.

One useful way to use the Enneagram is to start recognizing the patterns of fixation not only in yourself, but also in your relationships. Forgiveness and compassion become possible when you discover that each one of us is simply wired a little differently, each having a different process for completing the same task. Recognizing your mother's egoic structure gives insight into what may seem to have been inexcusable behavior. With this understanding, we can begin to forgive ourselves, our partners, our parents, and our children. We can stop demanding that the people in our lives be different from the way they are. We can stop demanding apples from a pear tree.

Through the process of recognizing our patterns of fixation, something very important takes place. Conscious mind inevitably realizes that there is more going on in life than meets the eye. You may begin to notice patterns of behavior that were previously invisible. Tracing the origins of these patterns back to the core fixation begins a beautiful process of making peace with yourself on levels that you may not have known existed. As you gently unravel the knots blocking the full expression of your being, the subtlety of textures imprinted over time will undoubtedly amaze you. When we stop identifying with the mechanical patterns of ego fixation, we stop taking life personally, and the suffering caused by our reactions to life's experiences can end.

●   ●   ●

I suggest that you first read this book all the way through. As you read about each fixation, begin to generate possibilities of comparison with yourself, people you know, or famous personalities.

Don't worry about being right, and don't hold too strongly to your first impressions or opinions.

It is important to realize that we all manifest all the patterns at one time or another. However, there is one place where we are fixated, one place that may be hard for us to see, one place that we subconsciously overlook in the certainty that we are not like that. It is also important to note that we do not change fixations. We employ strategies from all fixations, and we move to certain strategies under stress and certain strategies in relaxation. (Movements of the points will be discussed in greater depth later in this book.) However, the crystallization of the primary fixation never changes.

It is not the fixation that wakes up. You wake up from your belief that you are a fixation. But first you must identify your subconscious identification and face it before you can be free from it.

The Enneagram will reveal the subtle dynamics that show up in relationships. Be respectful with this system. Never use it to best your partner in an argument by saying, "Oh, that's just your fixation." If you say that in a polarizing tone of voice — and you must always trust your partner's feedback on this — you are lost in your fixation as well, and in no shape to point out others' deficiencies.

Some people will recognize themselves immediately when reading a particular description. Others will vacillate in doubt. Notice that doubt is the "passion" of point Six. Others will recognize themselves in all the points of view. It may take several readings to find yours. Hold it lightly and play with recognizing the manifestations of all the patterns within yourself and those around you.

The great potential of the Enneagram is that it can be used to cut your identification with the ego. You can discover that the ego is just a pattern; it is not who you are. Then you can allow your identification with ego to dissolve, refusing to fuel it with your participation.

Use the Enneagram as a vehicle for awakening rather than as a way of becoming a better "something"— a better Five or a better

Seven. Some learn the system in an attempt to find the right marriage partner or to improve their businesses. This is misusing the sacred Enneagram and only serves to perpetuate personal suffering; it does nothing to uncover the root of all suffering. The root of all suffering is identifying with one's fixation as if it were the reality of who one is.

The potential is to use the Enneagram as deep spiritual medicine. It is not about becoming a better fixation. It is about discovering who you really are beyond any pattern of thought, feeling, or behavior. There is nothing to do. All doing is driven by fixation. Thus, more doing is only fixation. The willingness to stop all fixated doing, to die to personal identity as a knower and doer, opens the possibility of recognizing what is here now, prior to any doing. Simply seeing the mechanical nature of the patterns you have identified as yourself allows for a deeper surrender and discovery of the truth of yourself.

Once you have seen through all false identification, it is possible to realize true freedom, to live as boundless essence of being rather than in the imagination of who you believe yourself to be. Free from imagining yourself to be who you are not, you will recognize your own Self everywhere. In this meeting with your Self, you are the silent embodiment of happiness and bliss.

• • •

HEALING ARTS OFFERINGS

INTUITIVE GUIDANCE SESSIONS 60 MIN – $275
with Deva Shantay

Through Deva's intuition, she guides you through the practice of direct intention to bring you back into alignment with your life purpose. Deva incorporates her knowledge of Yoga Therapy, Ayurveda, the Enneagram, Chakras and the Aura when appropriate. Each session is customized based upon the intention and needs of the client and may involve breathwork, meditation, movement, channeling, energy clearing, intuitive wisdom and/or past-life reading. Deva works both in-person and remotely.

SPIRITUAL READINGS WITH ENERGY HEALING
60 MIN – $185 | 90 MIN – $275
with Ann O'Brien

Ann uses her intuitive abilities to see energetic patterns in your life, so you can release blockages and fulfill your destiny. A session with Ann will empower you to find peace and clarity around relationships, work, and other matters. She works with healing guides to assist you in releasing stress, unhelpful habits, and beliefs along with other people's energy.

AURA-SOMA SESSIONS 90 MIN – $200
with Jacqui Forster

Aura-Soma is a holistic wellness tool which helps you become the best version of yourself. It is created with the highest quality organic and biodynamic ingredients, and is a perfect addition to those seeking a healthier lifestyle, and a better understanding of themselves and the world. Jacqui has been working with Aura-Soma for over 20 years. She is a gifted facilitator who brings an attitude of service to the process, allowing you to feel safe and supported as you explore your reflection through the colors. During the consultation you will be guided through a customized self-selection session with the bottles and you will choose one of the Equilibrium bottles to take home and support the journey your soul is ready to embark on.

PRIVATE MEDITATION COACHING 60 MIN – $200
with Melanie Moser

Melanie offers one-on-one or partner meditation sessions for all levels. Each session begins with an intention-setting and leads into a series of practices that will support your individual goals as a meditator for peace, concentration, confidence and enlightenment. Practices include: pranayama, guided visualization, mindfulness techniques, and a host of other restorative methods to bring your mind/body into alignment.

HOLISTIC HEALTH COACHING 60 MIN – $150
with Kerrie Schur

Envision and create a clear path toward optimal health through holistic approaches to nutrition, movement, your daily routine (dinacharya) and overall self-care. With a compassionate, intuitive, and integrative approach, Kerrie offers guidance that will support you in cultivating a way of taking care of yourself that feels dynamic, empowering, and sustainable. During sessions, expect a warm and inviting space to share what's most important to you. She will discuss your personal goals, wellness concerns, and help you explore the best steps to tending to your body, mind, and soul. You can expect at least one actionable recommendation to implement and experiment with right away. Kerrie is available over the phone, Facetime, or Zoom.

HERBAL CONSULTATION 60 MIN – $185
with Sarah Morehouse

Plant medicine can come to us in many different shapes, depending on what we need at the time. Herbal healing can come in the form of teas and tinctures but also plant meditation ("plant sits"), dream-plants, and using culinary herbs for medicine. Sarah will help you identify areas of your life that can be expanded and supported in the realm of nutrition, overall vitality, supporting the immune system, spirituality, and daily life choices. Sarah's approach to holistic plant healing is focused on using gentle, wide-spectrum, and easily accessible herbs. You can expect suggestions for changes or additions you can start immediately as well as a more detailed offering of suggestions for plant medicine that is specifically customized for your body and life.

CONSCIOUS MOVEMENT PRIVATE 75 MIN – $125
with Emily White

Conscious Movement is an invitation to know your body better and refine the way you move through life. The session begins with assessing movement patterns to uncover any interference/compensation in your physical posture. Through conscious movements you will explore and gently work to unwind your overactive tissues. Once you have restored your body to balance, ignite the parts of your being that have been forgotten or neglected and give them a clear sense of function and purpose.

True Nature offers four luxury treatment rooms to accommodate*
your bridal party, baby blessing, or friend and family spa day.
Let us help plan your special day!

*Group bookings scheduled at least one month in advance.

TRUENATUREHEALINGARTS.COM | 970.963.9900

The Inner Essence of the Enneagram

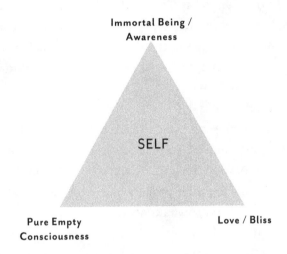

Immortal Being / Awareness

SELF

Pure Empty Consciousness

Love / Bliss

This simple triangle is the underlying basis for the structure of the Enneagram and all of Pythagoras' mathematics. Everything else unfolds from this trinity. The triangle represents the core aspects of the unnamable living truth that underlies all manifestation. Also called dialectics or trialectics or Taoist Yin Yang and Tai Chi, or Proton, Electron, Neutron, Gurdjieff described the Holy Law of Three: the Affirming, the Denying, and the Unifying. Pythagoras taught that out of the unnamable, unknowable, formless One, before number or universe, arises the Universal Mind and the Universal Soul. From this triangle, the universe emanates in mathematical laws of harmonics. These mathematical laws are immutable and unchanging and give rise to all movement and form.

To speak about the unnamable as an object is not accurate. The truth of being is not an object, form, or thing that can be named. Yet, in the search for the nameless truth, names can serve as fingers, pointing us in the right direction. Pythagoras preferred numbers for names and saw numbers, representing vibrational frequency, as the closest approximation we can come to naming truth, which is why in this book people can be referred to as numbers, representing the vibrational frequency of their fixation.

Different spiritual traditions use various names to indicate the absolute: Truth, Dharmakaya, God, Love, Buddha Nature, Self, Nothingness, Existence, etc. Pythagoras called it "the One before numbers." All these names refer to that same unnamable, immeasurable, eternal Presence, universally recognized in all cultures and traditions.

In Sanskrit, the Self is described as *Satchitananda*. The meaning of "Sat" is immortal being, which is also *awareness*. "Chit" can be translated as pure, limitless consciousness, which is absolute intelligent *emptiness* beyond time, space, and form. "Ananda" means *love/bliss*. These are the three primary aspects of the one indivisible truth and the first Pythagorean triangle.

Pure and unlimited Awareness, Emptiness, and Love are the true nature of what expresses itself as *I*. There is only one *I*, and this One gives rise to all of manifestation. Looking out through myriad eyes, the One sees its own reflection everywhere. Everyone says, "I am." This is universal. Who is there to say, "I am not?" When you see love everywhere, in all forms, this is not fixation but a taste of reality.

I have overlaid the three aspects of immortal soul, or Atman in Sanskrit on the primal Pythagorean triangle. In truth, these aspects of Self are indivisible and seamless; just as "heat," "light," and "burning" are not separate from fire. But for our purposes of inquiry, we will put these qualities on a triangle, and we will act as if immortal Being were somehow distinguishable from Consciousness and Love.

Another octave in frequency down we find Awareness, Intelligence, and Bliss which are qualities that naturally fluoresce as expressions of Being/Consciousness/Love. This is the true, radical condition of true Self.

You do not have to work on anything, create anything, or transform anything to become this. It is not as if someday, when you work hard enough, you will make it so. It is who you already are. The only thing telling you otherwise is your mind's identification with form instead of formlessness. The mind, because of its conditioning, creates veils of ignorance, fear, and desire, based on the idea, "I am somebody."

The perception of a "universe" is a trance induction. What the Hindus call the "veiling power of *Maya*," and Pythagoras called, "the imposing of limited on limitless". This trick of Maya makes it seem as if pure awareness is not all there is. As the Self plays this trick on itself, consciousness seems to be limited through identifying itself as form. This is Maya's illusion. In pure, white light, nothing is seen. In pure darkness, nothing is seen. Only in the interplay of shadows and relativity does appearance manifest. This is the magic light show of Maya.

Soul and Essence

Soul is consciousness crystallized into a subtle form. It is the arising of *I* consciousness as an ephemeral body. According to Pythagoras and to Ramana Maharshi, it is the soul that reincarnates lifetime after lifetime, searching for fulfillment, happiness, and God.

When the soul is not enlightened and is burdened with an egoic identity, it is called *jiva* in the ancient Indian language of Sanskrit. In this case the soul, or jiva, is the storehouse of latent tendencies and unfulfilled desires that take birth in a new body. The soul's identification with the body creates the egoic knot of character fixation.

The qualities of the soul's essence are described in the Sufi system of subtle latifas.[6] Each quality of essence is masked by a corre-

---

[6] *Essence*, H.A. Almas (out of print.) When I read Hameed's list of the latifas I immediately saw their relationship with the Enneagram and applied a Latifa to each fixation.

sponding quality of fixation. For example, the red latifa of shakti, or power, is veiled by the Eight fixation's use of personal power. The green latifa of kindness is veiled by the Two fixation's imitation of kindness with pride. The white latifa of purity is veiled by the One fixation's anger at impurity. The gold latifa of joy is veiled by the melancholy Four's search for joy. The black latifa of peace is veiled by the Five's attempt to create peace by withdrawing from contact with the outer world. The blue latifa of absorption is veiled by the Seven's search for bliss through outside activities.

The latifas of essence do not describe the truth of soul, which is completely empty of all form; even the subtlest. The living empty intelligence that is the truth of being has no color, no form, and no quality, yet it is the source of all form and gives flavor, texture, and color to everything. The latifas are the expression of the true character as soul densifies into incarnation.

As the momentum of character fixation is confronted by an unwillingness to act out the old patterns of veiling, fixation burns, and one's true essence shines forth.

True Self

If souls are like sparks flying out into the infinite night, then true Self is not only the sparks, but also the night, the universe, and the field that the universe arises in. The cosmic joke is that the soul is made of that which the soul is searching for: immortal consciousness. Enlightenment is to realize that who you are is this same immortal consciousness. God, soul, and universe are realized to be One.

It is possible to awaken from the trance of ego and the identification with form. This is to realize the true emptiness of all things. There is a clear seeing that nothing really exists! Nothing is all that exists! And this "nothing" is beyond description or words. When you realize yourself as the totality of empty, intelligent fullness, this is called enlightenment, or awakening from the trance of suffering.

The experience of awakening varies from person to person in depth, duration, and scope. Some experiences are short and shallow, and other experiences are vast and deep. The more the individual mind is willing to open to what is beyond the mind, the deeper the realization. The truth of what is experienced does not change. However, what does change is the mind's capacity to approach and apprehend what is beyond its power to comprehend.

Once the knot of egoic identity is cut, you are free. In Sanskrit, the jiva has become a *Jiva Mukta*, a liberated soul. Just as the Buddhists list the qualities of the various Buddhas and Bodhisattvas, beings whose lives are dedicated to the enlightenment of all, the soul matures in its deepening realization of its true nature. After the experience of awakening, a natural deepening occurs. This deepening occurs through tests and temptations that either draw consciousness back into identification or release it to a deeper level of established realization.

The final release is reunion with God. Discovering its true nature, which is beyond all form, the soul realizes itself to be the formless One. In Sanskrit, the Self as liberated soul is called *Atman*. Once the soul dissolves into union with the Beloved, the One Totality, it is called *Brahman*.

Brahman, or God, is the absolute unchanging field that gives rise to all form, including God, soul, and all that we call the universe. When identification shifts from a particular body, however subtle, to the totality of being that gives rise to all objects, the soul realizes itself as pure, limitless consciousness. This shift in identification is called Self-realization. In this realization, not only do you find that love is all that there is, but you also discover this love to be who you are.

• • •

WHAT IS EGO?

I, Me, Mine

The First Falling Asleep in Ignorance

Once the apparently particularized consciousness identifies itself with a body, this is ignorance. Ignorance, or ignoring what is really here, is a form of hypnosis. It is a kind of falling asleep. In Sanskrit, the sleeping quality of mind is called *tamasic*. This is thick, dark, cloudy, dull, stagnant mind, with characteristics like mud sediment or used motor oil collecting in a pan. The tamasic quality of mind is ignorance. Ignorance first of true being, and then of mistaking oneself for a human being.

Ignoring true being is the root of all suffering. Out of this ignorance, fear and doubt arise: fear for the survival of the body, and doubt as to one's own competence in dealing with a dangerous world. Also arising are the desires and needs of the body. Love is veiled by the desire for love and the fear of being hurt. This leads to emotional armoring. In the perception that there are requirements for getting love, "selling out" occurs.

This is the human condition: ignorance, doubt and fear, emotional armoring, rage, the felt need for love, and performing in order to get love. This is a normal life; not a natural life, but a normal one.

The Structure of Ego

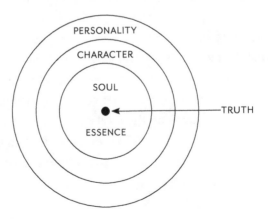

Personality

The outer, superficial layer

Every organism has a personality. We see it in dogs, cats, and horses. It has even been discovered and reported in E. O. Wilson's studies of ants. Personality is the most peripheral and superficial ring of the structure of ego. It is made up of patterns of either conditioned or genetic predispositions, which encounter environmental or social circumstances.

Personality involves the activities of the four bodies of manifestation — the mental body, emotional body, and physical body. "My thoughts," "my feelings," and "my body" are the three realms of manifestation with which people identify themselves. The fourth body is the situational body or the projected arena in which you play your part as if you are the center of the world.

The goal of most traditional therapy, starting with Freud, is to give you a more functional ego. Egoic identification requires the continual maintenance of a personal story. The story of *me* is made by stringing together distinguishing moments of arising phenomena and giving them a thread of continuity by taking it all personally. Therapy is often about changing the quality of the story that you tell yourself. The therapist is often a sympathetic coach who teaches you how to do the story differently. The coach is usually the one hired to boost your ego, while calling it self-esteem.

You *can* change your personal story. If you have a negative internal dialogue, it is definitely better to have a positive internal dialogue. Changing your story can be valuable at a certain stage. It can be important to know that you are not stuck in a particular story. If therapy stops on the level of personality, you will keep coming back to the same old issues, picking them up again and again, in similar circumstances, with a new cast of people playing the same old characters.

Often people come to therapy or workshops because they want to have more courage, get rid of fear, learn to be more self-accepting, or forgive their parents. All of that is working within the realm of personality change. The great trap in working on your personality and your circumstances is that the question of *who* has a personality, *who* is doing the work, never gets addressed.

Personalized story-telling is a form of self-hypnosis. It is a "trance induction" that consciousness puts itself into as it describes the world, reacts to the world, and develops personal opinions and beliefs about the way the world should be.

If you are spiritually ripe, you are not satisfied with just having a better personality or a better life. You are hungry for something deeper. There is a longing to return home, a longing for true peace, freedom, and love. Fundamentally and ultimately, the personality is neither the problem nor the solution.

Character Fixation

Deeper than personality, the Enneagram is not a system of personality, as it is so often presented, but rather a definition of character fixation. The same character fixation can manifest across a full range of personalities. Bill Clinton and Joseph Stalin have the same Eight character fixation, but vastly different personalities.

Character fixation will be found to be genetic. It is a successful strategy for group survival to have genetic predispositions for different roles. Some are warriors and some scouts. Some nurture family and others go off to explore the unknown and all enhance the group survival, which means the genetic survival. This goes on at a level deeper than personality. This is where the knot of ego resides. All thoughts, feelings, and behaviors of the personality arise from this core identification. Character fixation can also be seen as the central strategy for survival of the body and the family. It is at this level that the false sense of "me," which is the root of all unhappiness, can be recognized and transcended.

True Character

Qualities of soul

Character fixation is the egoic masking of *true* character. True character resides at the level of soul. It is the expression of the qualities of the soul's essence developed over lifetimes. True character is developed when one is willing to sacrifice personal pleasure or safety for something more important, to stand for what is known to be true in the face of the fears and rationalizations of the character fixation.

Working directly on true character never develops it. This would be a form of selfishness. True character is exposed and strengthened in acts of selflessness.

The great challenge is to recognize and expose the character fixation's *imitation* of both true character and the essential qualities of soul, described in the next section. This imitation becomes intrinsic to the ego's strategy for obtaining a sense of safety, control, and love.

Character fixation also helps to keep the sense of *me* safely unexamined by providing a positive image to identify with, whether overtly or secretly. Each fixation has an "idealization," an internalized story that makes it seem good and right and covers what is really going on.

When you first encounter the Two, or "giving," fixation, it seems so loving and friendly. "How can I help you, and what can I do for you?" is the implicit message the Two transmits. However, when you get to know this fixation a little deeper, it seems more like an extraction machine. "I'll take care of you, if you give me back love. I'll do everything for you, if you give me my self-worth." This hidden selfishness is covered by the imitation of true kindness. True, essential kindness needs no recognition, whereas the egoic imitation of kindness needs to feel recognized.

Because it imitates the essence of the soul itself, the character fixation can feel like a very real experience of who you are. For this reason, the sacred Enneagram is a ruthless aid in its capacity to penetrate through this trick of egoic mind.

I Am Somebody

The birth of the ego

Once the first thought of *I* arises in the empty field of consciousness, there is identification as a body. People say, "I am Fred, and I am forty years old." The identification is with the body. Once the thought "I am somebody" arises in pure consciousness and identifies itself as a particular body, then the triangle looks like this:

With the thought "I am somebody," the universe as "other" also arises. There is no distinction of you, he, she, or it, without first having an *I*.

Once there is an *I* and a world, then it follows that who one is, is inside, and the world is outside. This is the primary alienation of ego. All suffering arises from this sense of a separate self.

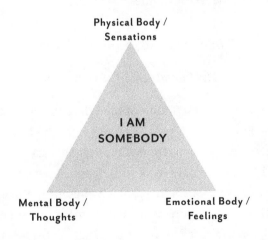

Physical Body /
Sensations

I AM
SOMEBODY

Mental Body /
Thoughts

Emotional Body /
Feelings

The myth of Adam and Eve is full of the symbolic resonance of the path of consciousness towards its own awakening. In the

Garden of Eden there is oneness, and the human is still unself-conscious. God, the creator, then gives a commandment to not eat from a certain tree. In order to eat from the fruit of this tree, the mind of man must challenge God. The temptations of the flesh are used to overthrow God. Eating the fruit from the Tree of Knowledge of Good and Evil symbolically destroys the oneness of the Garden of Eden, and the duality of mind appears — man vs. God, man vs. woman, right vs. wrong, shame vs. pride. Now humans are cast out of the Garden and wander for untold generations with the mind in charge and at war with God. The result can be seen on the Earth today.

The *I* imagines itself as the doer, the thinker, and the enjoyer. This is the identification with the physical, mental, and emotional bodies. In this way, the egoic mind has now assumed the place of God, imagining that it is in control. Every ego feels that it is the one in control and secretly realizes that it does not have a clue as to what to do. When the suffering of this condition becomes unbearable, the prodigal son returns home to the source. The mind returns in surrender to God, and individual consciousness finds its way home to the divine.

The Crystallization of Fixation

The formation of the knot of ego

The Enneagram is a description of the *I* thought that is the knot of ego. The Enneagram is usually taught from the viewpoint that fixation is a personality phenomenon that appears at a certain point in childhood. In my work with people, I have found that the fixation, or its predisposition, is already present in the womb. It is true that there is often a remembered moment of crystallization in childhood, around three to five years of age, as the ego structure becomes developed. Though the fixation may become crystallized at that time, the potential for it was latent, waiting for its moment to appear.

We might see this like a flower. Even before a rose blooms, it is obviously recognized as a rose. The potential of the rose flower is inherent in the seed. The flower will bloom in its proper time. Similarly, the character fixation is already evident in infancy and some fixations also seem to share common womb memories.

There are certain physical manifestations unique to particular fixations. In studies with twins, and in my own observations, I have noticed that identical twins seem to have the same fixation while fraternal twins seem to have different fixations. This would again point to character fixation being rooted in the DNA.

One fraternal twin reported her memories of being in the womb:

I have the Five fixation, and I could not stand having my sister in there with me. It was so claustrophobic. I have spent the rest of my life running away from that experience to be alone in solitude. My sister, on the other hand, a Two fixation, loved having company in the womb and still continues to chase me down as I travel around the world hiding out.

When I asked my teacher about the root of fixation, he said it is the unfulfilled desires that take birth. These unfulfilled desires or latent impressions, called *samskaras* in Sanskrit, are what arise as character fixation in birth. The ego forms and takes shape in order to fulfill those desires. This is what is known as *samsara* or "the endless cycle of suffering on the wheel of incarnation."

Childhood

The setting for fixation

When we are babies, we experience our parents as God by every definition of the term. Just consider what "God" means. God is the Creator, God is the provider, and God is the all-knowing. Parents fit that definition for the baby. Since the parents created the baby, the baby literally experiences them as the Creator. Parents are the providers: without the parents, the baby dies. And, from the baby's perspective, the parents are all-knowing: they go outside and visit other worlds the baby has no concept of.

Unfortunately, most of us are born into a world in which God, the parent, isn't enlightened. We come into the world as pure awareness, totally dependent on our parents. God, the parent, then gives us a name, says we are a body, and soon we have a past and a future. The parent as God passes on the trance induction of slavery. We are stamped with a personal identity; this is the primary wounding. Instead of being recognized for who we are as pure consciousness, we are recognized as either good babies or bad babies. If we sleep all night or eat on time, we are good babies. If we get up and cry, we are bad babies. Perhaps we are pretty babies or ugly babies, smart babies or stupid babies. These are the super-impositions of the world, of "God" telling us who we are.

The trance induction of our name starts immediately. How many times, over how many months, do we hear the repetition, the weaving of the spell: You are "Sally." Finally, it is internalized, and we agree, "Yes, I am Sally."

Given that this is the conditioning, the little baby has to learn how to survive. Therefore, the baby learns its individual program — how to smile and be cute, or how to fight against the program. The baby learns that to be a good baby is to get love, and to be a bad baby is to get rejected. Although the styles may be different, both are relationships involving parental conditioning as the survival mechanism.

At this point the child has lost touch with who it really is. It is identified as a body, with built-up armor, defenses, and behavior patterns. The child believes, "This is me." Then the child goes out to find "happiness, peace, and fulfillment" in the world of objects:

"If I find someone who'll love me enough, then I'll feel good." "If I'm rich enough, then I'll feel good." "If I have the right partner, the right experiences, or the right clothes, then I'll feel good."

While believing oneself to be an organism streaming toward its inevitable death, this search outside oneself does not reveal the meaning or fulfillment hoped for in the search.

Searching in outside phenomena for peace, happiness, and love happens because one has fallen asleep in ignorance of one's true identity. The futility of searching outside for what can never be found there normally results in some degree of depression, paranoia, and emotional armoring. Once you are lost in the sleepwalking trance called "me and my life," it can seem like an endless cycle. Emotional armoring reinforces dissociation, which in turn supports doubt and fear, making numbing sleep seem desirable, and fueling the hunger for love from someone outside yourself.

The possibility is to start unraveling the cycle by turning away from the endless pursuit of fulfillment outside of yourself. Then you can begin to discover that the only way to true fulfillment is by going towards yourself into the very depths of your being. This is inquiry into yourself.

Eventually you come face to face with the knot of ego, the primal "me." This is the point of true surrender.

•　•　•

PART II

THE ENNEAGRAM
OF CHARACTER FIXATION

The Enneagram of Character Fixation

Those who mistake the appearance for the reality,
the shadow for the substance, and the true for the false,
fail to attain the essential.

– Gautama Buddha from the Dhammapada

We are now going to carefully examine the appearance, the shadow, and the false. It is the false self called "me" that has been believed to be the true reality. In seeing through the false, the truth is revealed.

For this examination of who you are not, we turn to the Enneagram, which describes the structure of character fixation, or ego.

The word *Enneagram* comes from Greek and means "nine-sided." The Enneagram of Character Fixation is a way of identifying nine different egoic masks. These nine masks of ego are clustered into three primary classifications, depending on which "body" houses the identification. When the identification arises in the physical body, the fixation is anger-based. When the identification arises in the mental body, the fixation is fear-based. When the identification is in the emotional body, the fixation is shame-based hysteria. These three primary fixations are all based in fear: fear of anger, fear of love, and fear of fear.

Within each of the three basic classifications — anger, hysteria, and fear — there are three different versions. There are three anger points, three hysteric or "image" points, and three fear points, which make up the nine basic types.

Character fixation in itself is not the problem. The problem occurs when the fixation machine is running and it's taken personally. Once you start to recognize the fixation as a machine, you can let go of any personal involvement. This personal involvement is the ego. When personal involvement is gone, problems are gone.

Fortunately, once we recognize that what we are calling *me* is just a pattern (and there are hundreds of millions of others who have the same pattern), then we can no longer take it quite so personally. We may then choose to stop identifying with the pattern. If one is firm in the willingness to not indulge in false conceptions of self, then one dies to the unreal and lives in the revelation of true being.

The Three Core Fixations

Each ego is experienced as the center of the universe, and people imagine themselves to be in control. The thinking mind believes that it is in charge; it makes things happen; it keeps the body safe. You may get quite upset when someone starts to tell you what to do. The impulse to rage is physical; it is an animal anger. It comes up in the physical body in the same way that the need for love comes up in the emotional body, and the internal dialogue comes up in the mental body.

Since "I" believes it is a body among many other bodies, alone and separate in a vast universe, then anger, fear, and needs arise. There is anger over who controls the body, fear about the body's survival, and identification with the body's emotional needs. These are called the core points in the Enneagram and are assigned the numbers Nine, Six, and Three.

9 – Anger

ME

6– Fear and doubt

3 – Hysteria and neediness

The Three Bodies

Physical, Mental and Emotional

Aristotle described humans as three soul/mind creatures. He saw that we first had a vegetative mind which controls keeping the body alive on the level of temperature, breathing, and circulation. We call this the physical body.

He said from this vegetative state the next level arises as the animal mind. This is what we would call the emotional body. It is the place of feelings – from attachment to rage, from fear to desire.

Out of the animal mind arises the human mind which he calls Reason. We call it the mental body. It is the capacity to reason without emotion and make rational decisions that mark humans as the next level above animal in Aristotle's view.

A fixation is only possible if there is identification with the physical, emotional, and mental bodies. As long as that knot is tied, and consciousness momentarily believes itself to be form — subtle or gross — the fixation is crystallized in one of the three bodies of manifestation.

- Three of the nine points of the Enneagram are fixated in the physical body. These points of view are classified as obsessive-compulsive, or anger points.

- Three points are fixated in the emotional body and are classified as hysteric, or image points.

- Three points are fixated in the mental body and are classified as paranoid-schizophrenic, or fear points.

We each have a physical, emotional, and mental body. We manifest most of the patterns of all fixations. Yet, our core point of view crystallizes in one of those three bodies more than the others. This is the location of our chief feature, the one place where our response to the world is most deeply entrenched. Each body seems to have its own mind and its own process of thinking.

The physical body thinks in the realm of impulse, moving toward pleasure and away from pain. It operates at a pre-verbal, non-rational level.

The emotional body thinks in emotions, or waves of feeling; it is non-rational and often pre-verbal. The emotional thoughts are of neediness and trying to get approval and love. Then the emotional reactions of anger, hurt, and sadness come into play when emotional needs are not met.

The mental body is in the realm of thoughts and ideas. It is the home of internal dialogue. Usually, there is a schizophrenic commentary on "me" and "my relationship" to the outside world, and worry about what to "do."

An obsessive-compulsive (anger point) could be driving along the freeway lost in emotions of love or mentally composing a poem, but if someone cuts them off while they are driving, their body has an immediate impulse to rage. That is the fixation of the physical body. How the anger is then dealt with depends on personal development and personality.

• Obsessive-compulsives, or anger points, move against people.

• Hysterics, or image points, move toward people.

• Paranoids, or fear points, move away from people.

We will carefully examine the nine fixations one at a time, beginning with the anger points, followed by the image points, and then the fear points. Nine, Three, and Six compose the inner triangle of the Enneagram and are each a core point of one of the three bodies: physical, emotional, and mental. Of these three core points, there are two variations: the exteriorized version and the interiorized version.

- Nine is the core of anger. – Eight is the exteriorized version. – One is the interiorized version.

- Three is the core of hysteria. – Two is the exteriorized version. – Four is the interiorized version.

- Six is the core of fear. – Seven is the exteriorized version. – Five is the interiorized version.

The Three Animal Drives

The genetic survival machine

Every animal is run by three primary instinctual drives, for the survival of the species:

- *Self-Preservation:* survival of the individual unit.

- *Sexual:* reproduction of the individual unit.

- *Social:* hierarchy and roles of relationship for the survival of the herd.

As long as consciousness identifies itself as flesh, then these three drives mediate all of life. These drives run the fixation on a substrate below the level of passion. They fuel the fixation's passion, and until these drives are addressed, the passions of fixation will continue to run unchecked.

It is at the feet of these three drives that the rape and pillage of humankind, the destruction of all the kingdoms of nature, and the very destruction of the balance of life on Earth can be directly placed. These drives are sublimated into the egoic desire for happiness and acted out through the passions of fixation.

In our time and culture of personal identity the opportunity is to use life itself as the teacher in transcending ego. In this sacred work, we have been given the unique gift of the Enneagram for approaching transcendence in a completely fresh way.

Each fixation is run by a particular passion. Happiness is sought through acting out the passions in an attempt to fulfill one of the three lower drives. Happiness is erroneously judged to be the result of indulging in fixation, when in fact the result of indulgence may be short-term pleasure followed by suffering and neurosis. Each time the fixation is indulged, the belief in a limited entity is reinforced.

It has been rare for an individual to be willing to make the supreme sacrifice of refusing to indulge in the fixation. This is why Buddha is worshipped thousands of years later. Clearly, the awakening of one rare soul in a generation is not enough. The myth of the divine savior that will sweep in with an army of angels to save us from ourselves is no longer operative. Each of us, one by one, must be willing to make the leap from animal to divine.

Through the Enneagram, this is not a concept but rather a very concrete process for the transcendence of selfishness. The transcendence of selfishness is not accomplished by *doing* anything, but by the complete willingness to *stop* the doings of selfishness. It cannot be transcended by repression, denial, or "just letting go." It cannot be transcended by wishing fixation away, spiritualizing fixation, or using a thought like, "It doesn't really exist." Selfishness can only be transcended by not moving in the face of a tidal wave of fixated momentum.

As long as life is lived based on survival, sex, and social status, it is a life lived for "me." This is a selfish life. It is a life of relative fulfillment and relative pleasure. What is sought for repeatedly is ultimate fulfillment and ultimate happiness. Yet this can never be found in the arena of relative selfishness. To find where true fulfillment dwells, the arena of relative selfishness must be left behind.

Remarkably enough, complete fulfillment, deep peace, and true love are found in a selfless life. In a selfless life, true Self is found everywhere. In a life that is lived from an identity that is transcendent of fixation, true bliss, true love, true intimacy, and true fulfillment are discovered to be the natural overflowing of life itself. The life is lived fully - incarnate in enjoying joy and loving love with wisdom and integrity.

Recognition of the three drives and their unique characteristics, which show up at each of the points of fixation, is useful in two particularly different ways. First, knowing the underlying drive vastly helps in accurately identifying the fixation. We have all seen so many people who are mistyped. But when the three drives can be correlated to the fixation, then mistyping becomes more obvious.

Second, in knowing the drive, you know your own worst enemy. You know where you are most likely to sell out. Though each drive must be faced and burned, there will be one drive that will be the hardest to get past and the first to reappear to tempt you back into fixation.

The particular passion that runs the fixation feeds primarily off one of the instincts, and this instinct becomes dominant over the others.

- Imagine character fixation as a three-legged stool. All fixations have three legs, but one leg is shorter than the others. Since one leg is shorter, the stool is tilted towards that side, tilting the whole landscape. Each fixation tends to view the world from its own tilted position. The Self-preservation types can appear more nervous and tightly wound than the others. They spend more time worrying about questions of survival and security.

- A Self-preservation fixation will bring strategies for survival into the social and sexual arena and will choose partners who feed the Self-preservation instinct.

- Social subtypes often constellate around their family life, prefer groups, and enjoy the social milieu. They call home often and are involved with their parents and their children. They organize everyone at work to go to lunch together or orchestrate dinners for groups of twelve. They are the people most interested in status.

- A Social fixation will make sexual alliances that further the social status and use the social connections and family to deal with survival issues.

- A Sexual fixation will use sex to deal with financial and social issues.

- Sexual subtypes tend to prefer one-on-one relationships. They are charismatic with sexuality leaking through their eyes. They tend to have more relationships with the opposite sex than with their own, and their sexual plumage is more pronounced.

Obsessive-Compulsives:
The Anger Points

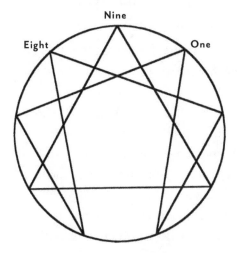

Anger first arises in the physical body. Other emotions and thoughts follow the anger. Their style is to move against people.

Sometimes called the "being group," the central issue for the anger points revolves around the mistaken belief, "I am only human." This is the first falling into ignorance. *Being* is identified as the human body. All problems, maladies, calamities, and suffering flow from this basic ignorance that has its root in anger.

The first and deepest rage is the rage of being incarnate in an animal form. Above that is rage at the Father for doing it to you. All other emotions follow from this core emotion of rage. Believing that "I am my body," and having suppressed both the primal rage and the blame of the Father, conflict arises between being "myself" and being controlled by others. This conflict manifests as patterns of defiance, control, and obedience.

Anger points misuse the energy of the mental and emotional bodies in service to the physical body's impulse to rage.

- The One is obedient, and therefore angry.

- The Eight is defiant, and also enraged.

- The Nine is trapped between obedience and defiance, vacillating between compliance, which produces rage, and noncompliance, which produces fear.

Core issues for all obsessive-compulsives revolve around time, dirt, and money. All three issues become arenas of struggle for control. For example, anger points can use the habit of being late to demonstrate non-compliance. Forcing others to wait is a way of maintaining control.

While Eights and Nines may appear quite unkempt — you may find piles of dirty laundry, old pizza boxes, and empty beer cans lying around — Ones are obsessively neat-looking. Everything looks perfect, and their clothes may take on the appearance of a uniform. Consider George Washington who designed his own uniform and emblazoned it into our American consciousness. For the Eight, tender and vulnerable feelings are avoided because they lead to dependency and weakness, thus a loss of control. Eights feel justified in expressing their rage, while Nines and Ones avoid rage as socially inappropriate.

Point Nine, the core anger point, is the root of all the other fixations. All fixations grow out of this first falling asleep into ignorance. In a sense, all fixations are versions of point Nine and eventually have to experience the awakening of the sleeping ignorant mind of point Nine.

Point Nine: The Core Anger Point

Essence:	Awareness
Holy idea:	Devine love
Holy path:	Right action
Chief feature:	Indolence
Passion:	Laziness
Idealization:	"I am comfortable"
Talking style:	Saga
Trap:	Seeker
Defense mechanism:	Self-narcotization
Avoidance:	Conflict
Dichotomy:	Believer / Doubter
Subtypes:	Self-preservation~Appetite Social~Participation Sexual~Union

While Nine is the core anger point, what is immediately notice-
able is the apparent absence of anger. Nines are afraid of their own
anger and so try to ignore it by being comfortable. On the surface,
Nines often seem to be sweet, easygoing, and gentle. They may
even seem to be flowing with the world. Since anger has been
avoided on such a deep, primal level, the surface symptom for the

Nine is an unwillingness to feel and express anger in the moment. Rather than feel the anger, they employ various strategies to ignore it or to go to sleep, thus replicating the original strategy of avoidance on a more superficial level of mind. It is much easier for a Nine to feel sad, lonely, frightened, or depressed, than to feel anger. The impulse to go to sleep to their anger is justified by the idealized image of a "loving person." Unexpressed anger may leak out through passive-aggressive behavior or build up to a point where the Nine may explode in rage over a minor event.

Positoned at the top of the central triangle, the Nine fixation has one leg in the conformist side of the Enneagram (One, Two, Three, Four) and the other in the nonconformist side (Eight, Seven, Six, Five). Nine is poised in ambivalence. One leg is in Three, which is the most conformist point, and one leg is in Six, which is an anti-authoritarian or nonconformist point.

The problem for Nines is that when they are compliant or conformist, it enrages them, and when they are noncompliant or nonconformist, it terrifies them. Because they want to be good boys or girls, they get trapped in compliance, resulting in rage. This may manifest as habitually agreeing with the preferences of others, and then passively expressing their anger about "feeling controlled," resenting the one who expressed a preference. This leads to Nines being emotionally isolated, slow to meet an agreement, or stubbornly holding onto their way of doing things. The first arising to any situation is an unstated, *No.* This impulse is immediately ignored with a smile and a *Yes, I would be happy to help.*

As one reported:

Don't tell me what to do. I hate being told. If you tell me what to do, I'll be like "ok," but underneath, really not wanting to be told what to do. I noticed this quite a lot in work environments, kind of wanting to do my own thing, I don't want to be told anything. In fact the job that worked the best for me was sales, because I could be a chameleon, and I was doing my own thing all the time, didn't have to have set hours or anything like that. It is much more comfortable, way more comfortable, than being in the same room as a boss every day.

Passion: Laziness

For the Nine, the core anger point, the passion that runs the machine is *laziness*. The Nine is unique in that all other passions are waves, whereas the laziness of the Nine results in the lack of waves. It is the sinking into turgidity and stagnation of not moving.

Nines are not necessarily lazy about working a job; they are lazy about working on what is essential. Anger and conflict are avoided at all costs. Rather than get angry, Nines become unconscious. Instead of engaging in the waves of rage, they sink into sleepwalking. The metaphor of couch potato describes a Nine's style of avoidance.

Indolence in Nines does not mean they are lazy people. They do work, and often they work very hard. They can be industrious and productive. However, they have gone to sleep to the essential issues in their lives. When an essential issue comes up, the Nine deflects into the nonessentials. You can tell they are getting close to something important when they become very involved in nonessential details. Nines report cleaning up for a big party when the house is a wreck and getting hung up on something like cleaning the grout in the fireplace with a toothbrush. They can focus on the details and forget the larger mess all around them. In ignoring the big picture, everything takes on equal importance. And, since everything has equal importance, all is done sequentially.

Imagine that you walk into a front yard and see that the lawn is half-mowed and the mower sits by a ladder at the side of the house. If you go up the ladder you might see that the window was washed, and then part of the desk inside was straightened, and there is a trail of half-finished projects, one leading to the other — and the teakettle is about to burn up on the stove. This is the Nine wandering from one unfinished task to the next.

A Nine reported that she was running late for a very important appointment. On the way out the door, she noticed her son's bed wasn't made. She went in to make the bed and got engrossed in a *Junior Scholastic* magazine article. She sat there on the half-made bed and read a grade school magazine, even though she was late for an important job interview.

Nines tend to be fascinated with structural aspects as a way of deflecting into nonessentials. This can make them good carpenters, electricians, or plumbers, since they can visualize behind walls to see the structure. It can also be a strategy to avoid listening to their wives telling them what is wrong with their relationship.

Avoidance of Rage

All Nines have issues of unresolved rage. It's always there. Quite often, they feel that if the rage was ever allowed to come out, it could become lethal. Rather than letting this happen, they go unconscious. A telltale sign of the Nine fixation in action is when they glaze over and "space out" instead of getting angry in the moment. A person who is often confrontational, belligerent, and pushy is not likely to be a Nine.

As mentioned previously, Nines hardly ever seem to be angry, despite the fact that Nine is the core anger point. They often appear very mellow. You really feel their sweetness. Because self-esteem is a real problem, these people will do everything they can to be loving and well-liked.

Ronald Reagan is a good example of this. Everybody around him said he was a nice guy. Everybody liked him; there was no sense of malice. He preferred being on his ranch, riding his horse rather than making decisions of state. There is a real sense that Reagan was merely a reflection of the beliefs and opinions of his strongest advisors (such as his wife or the attorney general). And he apparently rarely made decisions; everything was done by consensus of his advisors. He even claimed to be largely unaware of many of the important decisions that were made in his office.

Certain fear points are afraid to get angry and may consider themselves Nines. However, for the fear points, suppressing anger is in service of personal safety. They can be afraid that if they get angry, the response from the other may be violent. Nines are more afraid of their own suppressed violence. I have often had Nines tell me that they are afraid if they ever really let go they could kill someone.

This is not to say that Nines never get angry or that they never show it. They do. But the expression often comes much later than the moment that generated the feeling. There are blowups, but usually they are unrelated to the issue at hand, and often not directed at the offending target, but rather vented at a safe partner. Since anger doesn't get expressed appropriately in the moment, it builds until something minor or inconsequential sets off a volcano of rage that has been stored for years.

Losing a personal position

Nine is a special point in this system. It is the reflective point for the whole Enneagram. All the other points in the Enneagram have a distortion in their filters of perception created by waves of passion. Since the Nine's point of view isn't distorted, it can reflect all points of view. These are people who can understand and take all positions. It is difficult for Nines to know their own opinions because they can hear all points of view and everything sounds reasonable. For this reason, they can make good mediators, and were often the mediator for their parents when they were children.

A very sweet social worker reported having that problem. His superiors would say to him, "It's quite clear that this child should not stay in this home for all these good reasons . . ."

The caseworker would agree, "Yes, that's right. He shouldn't stay in that home. That's right."

Then he would drive an hour to the home, talk to the parents, and inevitably, they would say, "No, no, he should stay here," and go on to give all their reasons. The caseworker would understand and see their point of view, agreeing, "Yes, that's right. That makes sense."

He reported having driven back and forth for days, hearing and agreeing with all sides, unable to face conflict or confrontation. To take a strong position that others might not like was unthinkable.

People manifesting the Nine fixation have lost their own personal position and can see everyone's point of view, so their tendency is to take on the coloration of those with whom they share a relationship. Sometimes you will see Nines make radical shifts in style to blend in with new partners or a new environment. Ronald Reagan is a good example of this, again. He started out in a very liberal position in the Screen Actors Guild until his new wife took him into conservative company.

As one person reported about blending in to whatever the environment presents:

I am a chameleon, very much so, whatever my environment is. I have been with CEOs, in boardrooms with crystal glassware, and multimillion dollar deals in the afternoon, and in the evening I am in a punk bar smoking a cigarette and downing a few martinis and just fitting right in. I mean, those people would have no idea that in the morning I was in a boardroom with a bunch of execs. And I fit in with either environment.

A Nine reported being married to an Eight for over forty years. During that time he drank a bottle of whiskey with her every night and frequented drunken parties. His wife died when he was in his seventies, and he remarried an upstanding church lady. Now they rarely drink, except the occasional cocktail, and they go to church every Sunday. A completely radical change in behavior took place after a lifetime of alcohol abuse, based solely upon the patterns of his new partner.

Nines often take the subordinate position in a relationship to make sure they don't do anything that isn't perceived as being good. They seem to be able to melt into the other, to become a reflection of the other. Quite often, they end up with partners who act out more than they do, or partners who are emotionally volatile. The Nine is the reflector, the supporter in the background of the relationship.

It is rare to see a Nine leave a relationship. Either the other person breaks it off, or somebody comes and steals the Nine away. Nines find it very difficult to confront their partner directly. For them to take a stand, and to maintain that attitude long enough to actually make the split, is very rare. The way a Nine leaves a relationship is to shut down emotionally and become wooden until the other one leaves.

One woman reported:

You asked the other day if there was a time when I would have said, "Yes," when I really meant to say, "No." And forty-five years ago, when I was standing at the back of the church, about to walk down the aisle, I didn't want to go down the aisle. And I remember—I can still feel it in my body—that I just didn't . . . I guess it was in the 60s, people got married. It was sort of expected. . . but I really didn't want to marry this person. He was a really good guy, nice guy, would have been really good as a good friend. The dilemma at the back of the church, "How was I going to just say 'No?" I wanted to say "No." Everything inside was saying that I should say "No." And eighteen years later, I said, "No." I called it, called it off.

About four or five years into the marriage I said to my husband, "Something's wrong here. I think we should talk." And he said, "Oh, there's nothing wrong here." And I said, "Well, I don't know, I think we should clear the air or something." And he said, "There's nothing wrong here." So then he just walked away and reached for a beer, and went down to look at TV. So, then six, seven years later, same thing. [laughter] So I said, "I think we really need to talk." [laughter] I said, "Something's not right. Well, I think people argue. I mean I hear, I really hear that people throw things. It's supposed to be healthy." And he said, "There's nothing wrong . . . everything's okay here." So, same thing, reached for a beer and off he went. Then the next time around, it was a very, very strange thing, because the same routine, always the same everything, and one day he was coming in, the same time as usual, and I was making supper. Totally out of the blue, as soon as he walked in the door, I said, "I'd like you to move out on September first." And he said, "Okay." And he just passed through the kitchen, went upstairs, took a shower—the same as usual. September first he found another place, and that was it. There was never any anger, never any rage, nothing. Everything was dead. [laughs]

Control

Nines attempt to get control by holding on. Nine is the place of compulsive retentive behavior. It often shows up as collecting things that may be useful someday. They aren't collectors who give careful thought to the articles that they accumulate, nor do they review and reorganize their collections. Nines frequently have garages full of big boxes of stuff that they're "going to get to someday."

Their style of interior decoration tends to be like an Austrian beer hall, with beer mugs of all sizes and shapes and little relics everywhere — and all collecting dust. There may be an extra car engine or two in the garage, or every textbook since the first grade stored in boxes in the guestroom, or drawers full of odd-sized nuts and screws. Often, wherever the Nine is used to sitting, there are piles of newspapers or magazines marking the spot.

One woman reported that after the death of her mother she was cleaning out the attic and came upon an old desk filled with small drawers. In one drawer was a pile of string with a note, "String too small to use."

In their business lives Nines may find it very difficult to part with money, and they may be habitually late for appointments. Both are expressions of the tendency to anal-retentiveness.

Personal cleanliness can also be an issue. In India, a Nine country, I have watched people furiously scrub themselves with water from a river filled with filth, while squatting next to piles of garbage and manure. I once watched a woman sweep a portion of a dirt road. She created swirls of dust higher than her head as she moved the garbage from one spot to another, while water buffalo followed behind her, browsing through what she had stirred up.

Self-inflicted Injury

The holy idea of Nine is divine love, and the ego often uses this concept to justify its fixation. Nines really want to love and be loved. They believe that in order to be a loving person, and to be loved by another, they can't express anger. Unexpressed anger gets turned into passive-aggressive inaction, or self-inflicted injury. The body of a Nine may take on a wooden quality, as if years of unexpressed anger were stored in the tissue.

One woman told a story about her father, a Nine:

My mother was called out of town unexpectedly, and my dad was left with six kids. Nobody was doing the dishes. So after a few days he went into the kitchen and started washing the dishes. He was angry that no one else was doing it, but he never asked any of the kids to do it either. He was angry, and this anger was continually present, but he never expressed it.

While washing the dishes he crushed a glass and cut his hand. My sister had to rush him to the hospital where he had to have several stitches. When he came back from the hospital with all these stitches, and the dishes still weren't done, he didn't say anything to any of us. Instead he went back into the kitchen and started washing again. In a short time, he had crushed another glass cutting his other hand, and he had to go back to the hospital again.

As this example shows, certain Nines can display anger by deflecting it onto themselves. Consequently, they are often accident-prone and bump into things. Insurance companies have found that a vast majority of all accidents are caused by a small percentage of people. Most of them are probably Nines, who tend to "check out" of the body as a way to avoid feeling anger.

An electrician described that when he took his kitten to work with him, it ran into the street and got run over when he wasn't watching. Angrily, the man turned and walked into a tree branch, nearly putting his eye out. This Nine didn't know what to do with his anger, so he turned it inward. He perceived this event of walking into a stick and almost poking out his eye as punishment for not keeping an eye on the kitten.

A friend of ours who is a Nine has flipped his car over at least two or three times driving down from his mountainside home. He has a habit of getting in his car and driving when he's angry, sometimes losing control. Nines often express their rage while driving because it is depersonalized. They can scream, mutter, curse, or speed, enclosed in the anonymous shell of their car.

Childhood Setting

It is common for the Nine to describe a trauma in the birth canal. There is often a feeling of pressure and a desire to fight against it, as well as a feeling of being closed in. Experiencing pressure and feeling helpless to fight against it can cause Nines to become rigid and passive-aggressive. They may become immovable under pressure. There is a sense that it is futile to fight and resist. This leads to a deep sense of depression and despair.

This theme can repeat itself in infancy and childhood. One woman recounted that in her early childhood she was often given to fits of anger and crying. Each time she started one of these fits, her mother put her in the closet and locked the door. She said she would stay there until she cried herself to sleep. The message she got from this was never to express anger because anger led to isolation and darkness. The only escape was sleep.

Another adult Self-Preservation Nine told me of his childhood in Germany. His home life was miserable and the only thing he looked forward to was Christmas. It was the best thing that happened all year long. One Christmas, his mother made identical wool suits for all five children. This Nine, who was five years old at the time, put on his suit and began to itch. The itching was driving him crazy and he wanted to take the suit off. His mother said, "You have to wear this suit to celebrate Christmas." He felt the dilemma of wanting to comply, while at the same time being enraged by the compliance. He thought, "I have to either wear this suit and suffer in order to have Christmas, or not wear this suit and stay home in bed." His mother tried wetting the suit to make it more comfortable, but it just made the itching worse. Now he had a wet, itchy suit. The man told me this story when he was in his forties, and he still carried that rage with him.

Another Nine told a story of an experience he had as a five-year-old. He was walking across a creek on a board when someone started throwing rocks at him from behind. He saw the rocks whizzing by, but he didn't know who was throwing them. When he got to the other side, he picked up a rock, turned, and threw it. He didn't hit the girl who had been throwing the rocks, but he hit her little brother in the head and it started bleeding.

Terrified that he might have killed the little boy, he rushed back across the creek and bandaged the child's head with his shirt. Then he ran home to get more shirts for bandages, terrified that the boy might die, and that he might actually have killed someone with his anger. When he got home, he ran to his room, opened the drawer, and grabbed the shirts.

His mother came in and said, "Where are you going? Unless you tell me where you're going, you're not leaving this room." He was caught between the terror that he had killed someone and the fear of telling his mother.

He chose not to tell her where he had been headed. Instead, he stayed in his room, raging and terrified. Compliance produced rage. From this experience, he decided to never get angry again, and to never express anger. Rather than get angry, he began to go unconscious.

As children, Nines were often in the background. They may have felt overshadowed by their siblings. The high drama was going on elsewhere in the family and the Nine was an observer. Often Nines describe acting as peacemaker in the family or hiding in their room while Mom and Dad fought. Many Nines say that expressing anger was simply not permitted in their family.

Although they were not center stage, Nines still had to deal with issues of compliance and rage. As children they tended to live through their parents, and as parents they tend to live through their children. Often these parents take their children to Little League or ballet, wanting them to do what they never did. Because the Nine tends to lose boundaries, there is the sense that if their child does it, it is the same as if they did it.

Idealization: "I am comfortable."

The idealization is, *"I am comfortable."* The essence that the Nine is veiling is "Being," which is imitated by being comfortable in the body.

Point Nine is the survivor point on the Enneagram. Nines can melt into almost any situation. In the passion of laziness, they avoid confronting the moment. This idealization of comfort is a way to justify not making waves. Selling out for comfort will often be one of the biggest traps for the Nine fixation. The tendency is to "let it slide." The temptation is to rationalize that what is happening now is not that important and can be dealt with later.

This report describing Reagan was written by Michael Deaver and published in *Life* magazine:

On the morning of the Inaugural, I arrived at Blair House shortly before 9:00 a.m. to help the Reagans prepare for the ceremonies. Nancy was getting her hair done.

"Where's the governor?" I asked.

Without moving her head, she said, "I guess he's still in bed."

I opened the door to the bedroom. It was pitch dark, the curtains still drawn, and I could barely make out a heap of blankets in the middle of the bed.

"Governor?" I asked.

"Yeah?"

"Well, you're going to be inaugurated in two hours."

"Does that mean I have to get up?"

Talking Style: Saga

Talking style is very important as a diagnostic tool in each of the fixations. The talking style of the Nine is *saga*. Nines often feel more comfortable when they are the ones who are talking.

If you ask a Nine, "How are you doing?" instead of getting a simple response, you get a saga, such as:

Well, I'm doing pretty well, although I'm a little hung over this morning. I went out with Joe, you remember that guy, I think we met him at what's-his-name's party, and we went to that place on Fulton — what's the name of that? Is it Fulton or O'Farrell? — So you know, then we had some cocktails and we met that other guy, you know, what's-his-name, and he told me this story. It seems that he was . . .

Not all Nines are like this. Some develop the habit of shyness, hardly speaking at all. But even when the shy ones start speaking, they can give you too much technical information, or get lost in tangents.

Nines feel the unbearableness of staying in the present, so they tend to narcotize that feeling by jumping out of the present moment, or conversation, and into the ozone.

Milton Erickson, the famous psychiatric hypnotist, was a Nine. His way of putting clients into trance was by hypnotizing them with his monologues. Erickson would create an endless saga that would not only put people in a trance but also subconsciously carry the metaphor for his work.

Another important therapist who used his Nine fixation as his style of therapy is Carl Rogers. In Rogerian therapy, the therapist is non-directive, merely reflecting to the client the client's point of view. To Rogers, the perfect therapist is a reflector.

The Trap: Seeker

The trap for a Nine is being a *seeker*. The pattern of seeking is a way of self-narcotization. For example, one Nine I interviewed would look at the microphone and try to figure it out. Rather than being involved in the discussion, he would be thinking, "I wonder if that microphone is connected to those wires, and if there's a condenser . . ."

Nines can go on for hours figuring out and internalizing the world. Sometimes they enjoy woodworking, particularly sanding. They'll sand for hours and hours and hours while they are lost in thought . . . working things out . . . working on the world . . . discovering how it all works . . . seeking the structure of the universe . . . or the secret of life.

Nines are people who can do monotonous work and dissociate for long periods, while still doing a good job. Here you may find weavers, or people who do computer data entry work that is very tedious and repetitive. They derive a certain comfort from it. They appreciate having their hands busy doing something useful while they "check out" of the moment.

In my work I have discovered that the trap of the seeker can also be a trap door — an escape hatch to the other side. When the entire life is given in the willingness to seek the truth, the truth will reveal itself. The fixation itself becomes the vehicle to be ridden to the shore of the end of suffering.

However, crossing to the other side means leaving the fixation and all ideas of "who I am" behind. It finally means stopping the search. When what has been sought is found, the greatest challenge will be to stop seeking for more or something else. There could always be deeper, but the act of seeking goes off on a tangent instead of going deeper and misses the essential.

Defense Mechanism: Self-narcotization

The Nine believes that anger is forbidden, or at least strongly judged and frowned upon. To be angry is to be neither loving nor lovable. Because they want to be "good," they use *self-narcotization* as a defense mechanism to numb the impulse to rage.

According to Webster's dictionary, a narcotic is "a drug that in moderate doses dulls the senses, relieves pain, produces profound sleep" and, "something that soothes, relieves, or lulls."

For the Nine, this soporific effect can be achieved in a variety of ways. Although the drug of choice might be food, alcohol, or television, the Nine typically has developed ways to internally achieve this lulling. A workshop participant described the following self-soothing autosuggestion:

When I start to feel anger in a situation, I quickly calm myself by saying to myself, "It's okay, calm down, everything is okay." This happens automatically. I see that I do this to avoid suffering, but it doesn't really work. I know the anger is still there.

When he stopped this strategy, and directly experienced the rage that he had been avoiding, he discovered the genuine release that he had been trying to find through self-narcotization.

The defense mechanism of narcotization is often expressed through habit and routine. A Nine who breaks a habit often feels as if he's lost a piece of himself. Nines rely on habits that enable them to go to sleep while the habits act as automatic pilots. These are people who may have the same breakfast every day, year after year. I once read a news story about a man who went to the same diner every day for forty-two years and ordered the same meal.

Occasionally, male Nines have appeared in my workshops who were old counterculture, LSD people. They were still wearing long hair, ponytails, and earrings during the yuppie years of the 80s when everyone else had moved on to designer clothes. Willie Nelson might be a good example of this.

The addiction to habit also means that Nines may be very successful business executives. Some are leaders of major corporations because they learned a pattern very early and then stuck to that pattern.

Nines often store their anger in their neck, shoulders, and bowels. They may develop orthopedic problems and commit self-inflicted accidents. I recently ran into an old friend who is a Nine furniture maker. He smiled and waved, bandages showing on three of his fingers and on his elbow.

Avoidance: Confrontation

Nines will *avoid confrontation* at any cost. One way they express anger is by just sitting still and doing nothing, digging in their heels. They can be the most stubborn people on the Enneagram.

Because Nines want to be loving and avoid conflict, it is extremely difficult for them to say no. Although they won't say no in the moment, as the commitment gets closer, they may seem to be wading through molasses. When asked to do something, their internal gut response often is, "I don't want to," while their answer is usually, "Okay, I will." But then when the time comes, they often don't follow through.

Nines may verbalize their anger in the safety of their family, or with pets, or fantasize about confrontation when they are in a non-confrontive setting. They will sometimes report how angry they were somewhere else, perhaps at work. Upon investigation, the other party often had no idea the Nine was angry.

A female Nine denied that Nines always avoid confrontation. "That's not true," she said, "I confront."

"Give me an example."

"Well, just last week I went in to see the boss and said, 'If you don't get that guy in the motor pool to start paying attention and be more courteous to people, I'm going to get really mad and give him a piece of my mind.'" She would never go directly to the source of the irritation, the man in the motor pool, and say, "You're making me mad."

The issue of the Nine is that anger does not get expressed in the moment, because often it is not consciously felt. Rather than feel angry, the Nine deflects into some form of self-narcotization.

Once again, Deaver on Reagan:

I walked in on him one morning shortly after the Reagans had gotten a new puppy, a huge, shaggy, Belgian cattle dog named Lucky.

Frankly, the dog drove me nuts. Keep in mind that I would have been at the White House since six in the morning, with one of two meetings behind me, and a full agenda to discuss. And the President would be in the Oval Office, with his dog, trying to teach obedience.

I would cough and suggest that we really needed to get going. He would pretty much ignore me. "Here, Lucky. Here, Lucky."

Finally, frustrated on that particular day, I said, "Mr. President, you need to get that dog out of here. He's going to end up pissing on your desk."

Reagan looked up and said, "Why not? Everyone else does."

The Dichotomy: Believer/Doubter

Each of the points has a dichotomy, a polarity. All fixations will manifest both poles, but they lean more toward one than the other. The dichotomy for the Nine is *believer/ doubter*. Some Nines are doubters with a believer in the background; others are believers with a doubter in the background. This dichotomy creates such circumstances as a ten-year "trial marriage." The Nine isn't really sure it's going to work out, so he'll continue to stick around for another couple of years until he's sure.

Nines will join organizations, but they may never fully participate. It seems they either believe in it but want to check it out, or they doubt it and want to check it out. They are never totally present in the moment. They seem to be believers, sometimes almost gullible about an idea, and the next moment they can be cynics who doubt everything. (Doubt is related to stress and the movement into Six, which is where the doubt originates.)

As one Nine reports:

I'll really believe something, I'll be really passionate about something, get excited about it, and then the self-doubt will come in, and I'm thinking maybe this isn't such a great idea, this might be a lot of work, you know, especially if it's a lot of work, as that gets scary. So you talk yourself out of things a lot. You get great, brilliant ideas, a lot of brilliant ideas, but you suppress it, it might not work. So then there is some fear of failure in there too. So you believe one minute then you doubt the next.

Subtypes

Self-Preservation: Appetite

The Self-preservation Nine is called *appetite*. In the extreme, these are the 400-pound people who need extra-wide seats on the airplane. There are also many appetite or Self-preservation Nines who are quite thin and athletic-looking. However, they feel a sense of unfulfilled appetite in everything.

Appetite is used to try to suppress the feelings of anger, but it doesn't work very well. This makes them the most visibly irritable of the Nines. It also creates continual craving for that which brings temporary relief from the feelings of rage and despair. I have worked with obsessive-compulsive pornography and masturbation addicts who were Self-preservation Nines.

In less severe circumstances, these may be people who refer to their possessions as "toys" and express the frustration that they just don't have enough resources to have the newest or best toy.

For one client I worked with, his big toys were racing cars. All of his income went into building racing cars, but it was never enough. If he was building a Ferrari, it wasn't the best Ferrari. If he was rebuilding a Lamborghini, there was always a better one out there, and if only he had *that* toy, then he would be happy. That was his issue in life. There was a hunger that could never be fulfilled.

Often, when Self-preservation issues are raised, such as the rent being late, Self-preservation Nines will try to deal with anxiety or anger by over-consuming, taking in huge amounts of drink or food. The fellow who had to wear the itchy Christmas suit is a Self-preservation Nine. He had to wear the woolen suit in order to enjoy Christmas, which created compliance, which produced rage. Now, forty years later, he feels there is never quite enough, regardless of whatever activities he may be involved in. Whether eating, drinking wine, or making love, satisfaction remains elusive.

Here is someone describing her Self-preservation Nine fixation for us:

I have become a master of how to amass energy, huge amounts of energy, with as little effort of doing anything as possible. Now I know this sounds like laziness, on one level, but I don't move easily, and you can't get me out of the house, and you know, commit to committees and things like that. I thought I was choosing it consciously to basically not be squandering energy. I even have this agreement with god, that whatever energy I put into something, like if something is terrible and just rips me apart, that I get more out of that, and maybe it's on other levels, but that I always energetically get more than what it took to put into it.

What's underneath there is this energy of what feels like a ravenous monster. There is something that can't be filled. So let's just fill that mother, you know, whatever it takes.

I mean it sounds like the most terrible thing possible. Underneath that is this void– it can never be filled – this is the Self-preservation appetite part of it, no matter what you eat, and even if you are over-stuffed to whatever degree, that doesn't work; no matter what you do you can't work enough, you can't watch enough TV, you can't go to the movies enough, you can't have enough friends, you can't have enough of anything that actually makes a difference to somehow fill whatever that void is.

It is almost like a column, a dark column or void, and it looks like there is no bottom to it, and even at one point it looks like—oh, my god, there is like a monster at the bottom of this--and that's why it can't be filled, the monster is just hungry all the time.

Social: Participation

The Social Nine is called *participation*. These are the "joiners." This is where the secret doubter often comes in, creating people who seek social participation, yet hang back. Participation for them means hovering between deep involvement and total non-involvement.

This is exemplified by people who join the Elks Club, the Moose Club, the Lions, Rotary Club, the Bowery Street Boys, the Masons, and hundreds of other fraternal, social, service, and business organizations. Social Nines go to meetings but rarely become leaders in the organization. They hang on the fringes, never really present and never really dropping out. If you ask, they may tell you they still have some reservations about the organizations they belong to. It's like the ten-year trial marriage, only it happens within organizations, groups, and in social contexts.

In personal relationships there is a loss of self in the field of relationship.

A person with a Social Nine Fixation described it this way:

Comfort is very big on my list. In fact if I could spend the rest of my life comfortably, that's really the solution and the answer to my life. That's it, then I got it made. Then the least I can do the better. I just love the idea of having nothing to do all day long, on my couch. To me that's heaven. Nobody to answer to, nobody to tell me what to do, don't have to do anything, there might even be a hard-boiled egg in the refrig-

erator for later on, and to master the art of ignorance really (laughter), because there is a lot going on in here, and you know one day I'll have to face it. (laughter).

If I can just not feel it, that's like the perfect strategy, then there is no problem. I love comfort....

ELI: Does it really work?

No, no. Also living my life vicariously through all of my relationships, as if that is who I am. My relationships are more important than the well-being of this body, than the mental well-being, more important than actually having right action, having something beautiful to do. It's like the enslavement to the idea that I am serving others, that others are so important in my mind, you know, others are more important than me, and everybody's needs come first. Everybody's concerns are more important and at the same time having rage and resentment that I am not taking care of myself. You know, it is very strange, but something is being seen more clearly than it was before.

ELI: Yes. So you getting ready to meet it?

Yeah, yeah. (Yawns...Laughs). Tomorrow.

Sexual: Union

The sexual Nine is called *union*. Sexual Nines melt into the other. They lose boundaries more than the other Nines, in the sense of not knowing where "I" as this body ends and the other begins. They are so melted in, and feel such a complete loss of boundaries, that they can't extricate themselves. They lose themselves in the beloved. This is an unconscious attempt to return to a sense of oneness, transcendent of fixation.

However, instead of dropping the personal idea of *me* to directly discover unbounded, vast, no-distinction awareness, there is an attempt to melt this *I* into another in order to create oneness rather than to realize it. It is the fixation's attempt to simulate returning home.

Sexual Nines talk about unconsciously eating off their partner's plate without recognizing there is a separation. I have never heard of a Sexual Nine actually leaving a relationship.

After reading the above, a Sexual Nine told me that it isn't necessarily true. He said that he and his ex-wife are both Nines and they managed a divorce. I was quite surprised and asked how long it took to actually get the divorce after they knew it was over.

"Well," he said, "I guess I knew it was over about six years before it actually ended."

"Still, that's pretty good," I told him. "How long ago did this happen?"

He smiled sheepishly and replied, "Three years . . . although she hasn't actually moved out of the house yet."

Nines will usually be attracted to a strong personality, someone who has strong opinions or can emote for both of them. They then attempt to blend into oneness with that. A Nine described it as "giving my entire self over." It's as though there's a melting. "I don't know any longer which are my needs and which are your needs."

A Nine frustrated by such a situation said:

My body starts telling me when it's the last straw. Something just snaps. But it builds and builds before that, and everything contributes to it. Not demonstrating anger contributes to it. When I explode, I'm dramatic. I walked out the door one day and didn't come back for a few months.

Additional Exemplars

Nines can be scientists, presidents, actors, or machine workers on an assembly line. They are flexible and can meet the demands of the situation and still feel comfortable. Former President Gerald Ford, bumping his head and stumbling down the steps of Air Force One, exemplifies the Nine style. The cartoon character Homer Simpson is a Self-Preservation Nine while John Goodman playing an Eight is a Social Nine.

An excellent film showing the Nine character fixation is *Being There*, with Peter Sellers (a Nine) playing Chauncey Gardiner. While having no real opinions of his own and living in total emotional isolation from his situation, he is able to enter rapport with everyone. He is seen as a sage genius who ends up advising the President by obliviously talking about gardening.

The "Dude," Jeff Bridges, a Social Nine in *The Big Lebowski,* is the pot smoking, bowling, slacker.

Diane Keaton expresses a Nine fixation. She has done her best work when directed by Woody Allen, a Six. This is one of the strongest relationships in the Enneagram, with the Six animating and giving life to the placid Nine, as exemplified in *Annie Hall.*

Countries and Cultures

All cultures and countries exhibit fixations. Austria is a Nine country. During the cold war, Austria was caught between East and West, socialist and capitalist. Austria has an easygoing veneer that is very different from other Germanic cultures. There is more comfort and ease than is found in neighboring Germany (a Six culture), or Switzerland (a One culture). When Hitler invaded Austria, he was greeted by cheering crowds. When the Allies invaded, they were met the same way. Austrians can take all points of view, while going to sleep in the middle.

Nines cherish good food and alcohol, but they can be very tight with money. Austrians, coming from a Nine culture, have an expression about each other: "He can squeeze a shilling until the thumbprint shows." When asked about bathing or personal hygiene, many of the Austrians I have met considered a bath more than once a week to be bourgeois and excessive.

One summer I was teaching in an old castle in the Austrian countryside. The local church dominates the small town of Plankenstein, of which the castle is a large part. The church bells chimed every fifteen minutes, with different chimes to mark the quarter-hour, half-hour, and hour.

Unfortunately, the clock was ten minutes slow! Since the church bells were heard throughout the castle, we had to set our watches and clocks back ten minutes to be on Plankenstein time. India is an example of a social Nine culture. The way India deals with time, dirt, and money is famous perhaps the world over. Bureaucracy is a Nine phenomenon, and India has raised it to an art form with four carbon copies for every form and six rubber stamps for every transaction.

In the early nineties, we once stood in an airline arrival hall in New Delhi at 2:00 a.m., waiting with several hundred others to clear customs. (This in itself is not unusual, as planes and trains are commonly scheduled for 4:00 a.m. arrivals and 5:00 a.m. departures.) Three of the four booths were closed, and the only customs worker carefully took his time to read each and every stamp on every page of every passport he handled. After about an hour the crowd was hot, smelly, and tired. Several Indian business-men started shouting, stirring up a potential riot. In response, the other three booths were suddenly opened, and the sounds of rapid rubber stamping quickly echoed in the hall.

When I was last there, decades ago, the Indian one-rupee note was worth about three cents. When received from a rickshaw driver, pulled from inside his sweaty shirt, the one-rupee note is a filthy, damp, leathery piece of paper that has been folded and refolded into a tiny square many dozens of times. However dirty or wet or folded it may be, it remains legal tender. However, if the bill has the slightest tear in a corner, do not accept it. It will be regarded as worthless.

India runs by rail. Trains are the major transport system, and the trains, like the buses and the planes, rarely run on time. Often a train can be six or twelve hours late. Once, I saw a train leave a station fifteen minutes early! Pity the poor folks who got there just in time. Although in telling this story to an Indian he replied, "It was probably yesterday's train!"

Some friends once chartered a bus in Northern India to take them from Bodhgaya to Varanasi. The trip was supposed to take five hours maximum, getting them into Varanasi at four in the afternoon. But the trip took twenty-nine hours, finally arriving at about four in the afternoon the next day. This was not considered unusual by the locals; the explanation was heavy traffic.

Exemplars by Subtype

The lists of exemplars presented for all of the points are not necessarily accurate, as it is often impossible to know someone's fixation without personal contact. However, the following list is evocative of the flavor of the different fixations and subtypes. While reading these examples, notice a sense of the quality of energy evoked.

Self-Preservation~Appetite:

Sometimes displaying a tight jaw from holding anger, or appearing bristly, these can be the Nines who hold their anger closest to the surface. Here is one person's report:

I didn't start out with it apparent that I was a nine. I thought I was a seven and that I was handling the fear well. (laughter). Once I was busted on it. I recalled when my younger son was five years old, one time at the dinner table he said, "Why are you angry?"

I said "I'm not angry."

And he said, "You have an angry face."

Woody Harrelson, Homer Simpson (cartoon), Julia Child, Karl Malden, Ed McMahon, Art Carney, Rodney Dangerfield, Walter Matthau, Russian peasantry

Social~Participation:

This is the most Three-like subtype of the Nine fixation, where relationship, family, and networking are usually of prime importance.

Ronald Reagan, Gerald Ford, Kevin Kostner, Kevin Spacey, Nicholas Cage, George Burns, Diane Keaton, Bill Murray, Milton Erickson, Joseph Campbell, The Lions Club, India

Sexual~Union:

Often the most dreamy-eyed and softest of the Nines. The desire to merge into the other as "beloved" is expressed by this woman:

It's such a strong belief that the beloved is out there, and it is the One. And without that One, then I am cut off from the heart, from the self, from the source, from life, from love, from everything, actually. From being. It seems so real.

I am actually going through the process of having had a relationship end where I had a profound awakening years ago, and recognized the beloved was here. And Gangaji was the teacher and Gangaji was the beloved, and when I met this person, it got completely shifted. It was just like all of it, you know, the entirety of it just got shifted onto him. The beloved was outside of myself. So I had to hang onto him until the point of making myself sick on a physical, mental, and emotional level. Because if I lost that person, then I lost the beloved.

Morgan Freeman, Forrest Whittaker, Ringo Starr, Mooji, Jay Leno, John Candy, Dean Martin, Charlie "Yardbird" Parker, Captain Kangaroo, Jerry Garcia, Austria

Point Eight: The Externalized Anger Point

Essence:	Shakti / Cosmic Power
Holy idea:	Truth
Holy path:	Innocence
Chief feature:	Vengeance
Passion:	Lust
Idealization:	"I am competent"
Talking style:	Laying Trips
Trap:	Justice
Defense mechanism:	Denial
Avoidance:	Weakness
Dichotomy:	Puritan / Hedonist
Subtypes:	Self-preservation~ Satisfactory Survival Social~Friendship Sexual~Possession / Surrender

The Indulgence of Rage and the Misuse of Power

A goat-herding Bedouin tribe projected their egoic vision on to an Eight Fixation warrior God they called Jehovah. He took care of his own, his chosen people, and killed everyone else. "Wipe out everything alive" can be found in the Old Testament as a commandment from Jehovah to the Hebrews as they march through the desert to the Promised Land. Jehovah is a vengeful and jealous god. The Mafia godfather, an imitation of the patriarchal hierarchy of Jehovah, takes care of his extended family and considers everyone else his enemy. The difference is that Jehovah doesn't require that you kiss his ring, a bit of foreskin will do.

Nothing, at the time of writing this new edition, better publicly demonstrates the worst of the eight fixation than Donald Trump. A hedonist Sexual Eight, he is the Mafia don writ large. He is loyal to his family. The rules do not apply to him. He is the classic example of a grifter. His psychosis of narcissism shows us the horror that happens when neurotic ego fixation moves into pathology; where the lies are so pervasive that there is no longer a capacity to recognize the truth. The mirror of life is so filled with the self-absorbed image that there is no room for reflection, compassion or seeing the world as it is.

Not all Eights are like this of course, just the psychotically narcissistic. A former V.P. in the Trump organization described Trump's passion for blaming, which is an Eight characteristic: "In terms of taking the responsibility for the buck, he just would never do it. It's not in his DNA. He's never responsible. It is always someone else's fault."

Eight is the expanded or exteriorized version of Nine. While Nines have lost their personal position, Eights have a personal position on everything. Nines turn the anger back inside; Eights project it out into the world. Eights feel justified in their anger. They are the "blamers" in the world. Everyone blames somebody occasionally, but Eights do it compulsively. They take the burning sense of, "I am innocent! I didn't do it!" and use that self-righteous stance to blame the world.

Personal Power

Eights are misusing the essence of power. The Eight uses personal power as a tool to dominate the world. Eights are always willing to raise the ante, either to defend their own innocence or to protect an underdog from injustice. When their ego misuses the holy idea of truth, it becomes, "Don't give me any of your bullshit. I can detect bullshit. I'm interested in the truth." Yet, they are generally the biggest liars and bullies on the Enneagram. Eights are the "bad boys and girls" of the Enneagram.

Almost everyone considers his or her fixation bad news, except for the Eights. Often, upon identifying their own fixation, people say they would rather be something else. Not the Eights.

Male Eights generally love to hear and tell stories about themselves. A favorite Eight pastime is to brag about being bad or tough or surviving amazing odds. A mild example of this is former president Lyndon Johnson, a Social Eight, pulling up his shirt on television and showing the scars from his operation.

In our society in the past, female Eights may have had a hard time expressing their Eightness because it is not society's perception of how women should act. Some female Eights I know are so deeply socialized that on the surface the Eight fixation does not appear. Instead, they may appear confident, smooth, polished, and socially compliant to those who don't know them well. At home or work, however, they can be verbally aggressive and they are usually the boss, like Michelle Obama.

Sometimes you can hear a shout or a push in their voice. Kellyanne Conway and Sarah Huckabee Sanders are also current examples of the puritan side of the dichotomy, like Michelle Obama. However, they have different sub-types. Sanders is likely a Self-preservation Eight, Obama a Social, and Conway a Sexual.

Bette Midler, Roseanne, and Mae West are examples of female hedonist Eights who made a career based on enjoyment of a good time.

Generally, one of the diagnostics of Eights is in the eyes. They have a glare and sometimes a Neanderthal ridge above the eyes. Lee Marvin, Robert Mitchum, Jack Nicholson, and Josef Stalin all have it.

Eights tend to see things in polarities. They have little tolerance for shades of gray. "Either you're my enemy or you're my friend" is the way an Eight interprets others.

Eights have developed the psychic ability to see weakness. They avoid weakness at all cost. Since every Eight is hiding a scared, incompetent, emotionally dependent little child under the bluff of their armor, they have learned to spot your weaknesses and attack before you can find theirs.

One man reported:

When I was five years old my father stopped using the belt and started using his fist. I had to lie to stay alive. I became a proficient liar, and I only got better. I used to practice speaking with my voice down low so that I could be seen as a man. I would bully you and push you and walk you down any street that I wanted to walk you down. I would con you out of your shirt and commiserate with you the next day about the dirty dog that stole your shirt. You did what I wanted you to do, or you had anger in your face.

Being an outlaw, or a criminal, is a major theme for Eights. They often act out the most anti-authoritarian stance. Eights will follow only the laws that they believe are correct and apply to them. There is often some kind of outlaw activity in an Eight's history. Occasionally, there is real crime. Prison inmates are often Eights. Getting away with something can be a favorite fantasy.

As one man reported:

I like arguing and fighting because even if I lose I'm gonna win. I grew up in a peaceful, quiet suburb where there was no crime or violence, so I created crime and violence. I was the leader of the gang. I didn't choose that role, but if somebody is going to do something, it will be the Eight. The others will follow or not, but the Eight has the energy to get it started.

Eights can also be the hero-warriors, working for the good of others. Gurdjieff is a good example of this. He dedicated his life to helping bring people to enlightenment. Yet, when he needed money, he was not above catching local birds, dying them yellow, and selling them as American canaries.

In personal relationships, work, and social settings, Eights have a tendency to fill the space and dominate the situation. They are bullies and justify their anger.

Mexico, Afghanistan, Serbia, Israel, and Borneo all have tribal warrior societies and are examples of Eight cultures.

Passion: Lust

The Eight's engine runs on *lust*. This is lust not only in the sexual sense (although that is usually present in large doses), but lust in the sense of desire for over-consumption of life and living. If the issue at hand is sex, they will either make love excessively or be lusting for the next sexual encounter. It is very rare indeed for an Eight, particularly a male, Sexual Eight, to declare himself monogamous. Whatever Eights do, they do to excess. If the pleasure of the moment is eating, they will eat too much. They may die of cirrhosis, gout, syphilis, high blood pressure, or heart attacks.

The way Eights wake themselves up from the torpor of Nine is through lust, so they have a tendency to either be asleep or to go full blast. Eights have a hard time doing anything in moderation. The passion of lust or the trap of justice is what moves the Eight out of the Nine's self-deadening position.

Here an Eight is afraid that she might lose her passion to blandness, in the process of exposing and transcending the Eight fixation:

Blandness worries me. I'm worried about losing my lust and losing my gusto! Some of the people who are interested in freedom seem a little too . . . [laughter], like I want to give them a boost! I'm afraid to lose my passion for life, and for me meditation seems like a way to the "ease" that I want but also may lead to what I'm afraid of, which is losing my passion for life.

The following letter was in a "Dear Abby" column:

Dear Abby, My husband retired five years ago, and I still can't get him to slow down. When we ride in the car, he hollers at the person ahead of us because they didn't pull away from the stop sign fast enough. In the grocery checkout line, he grumbles because the lady ahead of us had to write a check. He wolfs his food down. He's halfway through his meal before I even sit down. When we're walking together, he's always three steps ahead of me. He says I poke along.

Now he doesn't have high blood pressure — it's way down — but mine is creeping up.

The woman most certainly is writing about an Eight. This is the person with the sign on the desk that says, "I don't get ulcers, I give them," or "I'm right even when I'm wrong."

The other two anger points do not express their anger this way. Nines believe that it is not loving to feel angry, so they go unconscious. Ones, on the other hand, experience their anger, keep it internalized and suppressed, and blame themselves if things do not go right. An Eight "knows" the anger is the correct feeling to have, and "knows" it is someone else's fault. No matter what is going on, they are able to rationalize or justify their own anger, their own violence. In fact, the more evidence there is that they are wrong, the louder they get.

Moving Against

Eights have an oppositional, adversarial approach to people. A friend of mine was a bright, sweet, gentle, Jewish, seventy-year-old psychotherapist when he told this story:

You know, I thought I was out of it. I thought I wouldn't do this anymore. But this motherfucker cut me off in traffic. I found myself getting out of my car, and I ended up going up and grabbing him through the window! And the whole time, even as I got out of my car and was moving towards him, I kept saying to myself, "Morty, you're not really doing this, are you?"

Morty wasn't someone you would think of as being hostile or violent, and yet when the impulse came up, he acted on it.

Eights have a retaliatory reaction called vengeance — "If you do it to me, I'll get you back." If they are not able to get you back at once, the hostility will be held as a grudge and will reappear as vengeance, best served cold.

Childhood Setting

In order to survive, Eights had to develop a hard shell. They had to grow up fast in order to take care of themselves. They were punished for things they didn't do, and they often got away with things they did do. This created a sense that laws are arbitrary. The Eight thinks, "I make my own rules, and I follow my own rules."

While Nines as children were pushed into the background, Eights were often physically or emotionally tortured, or felt that they were. Most male Eights tell of physical punishment in childhood. Even those who were not spanked or whipped often describe some other kind of torture. This is not always true with female Eights, who do not necessarily identify childhood as a violent time. However, more than one female Eight has spoken of being violently attacked and sometimes sexually abused by a father or older brother, or sometimes having to defend the younger children against a drunken, raging father.

At an early age, the Eight became convinced that the world is a jungle, and in order to survive you have to "get them before they get you." Eights feel that they were victims of injustice, so justice becomes a burning issue. They blame the world and are out to make it right.

Here, a female Eight talks about being falsely accused by her mother:

When I was little, my mother and I lived alone. We had a cat. My mother liked expensive perfume, and she had these perfumes on her dresser. Our cat must have got up there and spilled her perfume. I put everything back before my mother came home, but the place really stank from the spilled perfume.

As soon as she walked in the door, she started screaming at me about getting into her perfume. First of all, I couldn't stand her perfume. And I didn't do it, so I said, "I didn't do it."

"Well, who else did?" And she went on and on and on. I looked at her as she continued yelling at me and falsely accusing me.

I said, "Wait a minute." And I walked over and I slammed every bottle into the wall. I broke all of them. And what didn't break, I started smashing.

Next, I let her beat on me. I had a sense that if I ever hit her back, I would have killed her, because she was a very little person. So I thought, "Okay, I'm going to take the rap for this. But first I'm going to have the pleasure of doing it."

Idealization: "I am competent."

When they were very young, Eights experienced being overwhelmed by life. The moment of crystallization often felt as if life and death were in the balance. Since they survived this overwhelming trial, they developed the conceit that they could handle anything. Therefore, they are considered "street smart."

The Nine's idealization is, "I am comfortable." Regardless of how hard life might be in the moment, Nines will generally say, "Yeah, I've got it pretty good here. I've got my TV, my bills are paid, I get by, I'm okay." Their idealization is that they are comfortable; they don't have any real trouble in life.

The Eight's idealization is, "I am competent." They can handle things. An Eight describes her experience of being competent:

You can count on me. That's another thing that I enjoy about myself. If I say that I will do something, it's done. If I say that I am going to do something, there's no waffling. The saying of "I'm going to do it" means that it's done and there's very little time between saying that I'm going to do it and it being done. I have high self-esteem because I do what I

say I will, and I can count on myself. If I have a list of stuff to do today,
I'll do it, and that's all there is to it.

Because of this conceit and the need for stimulation to stay
awake, Eights tend to live on the edge. They drive too fast and can
be maniacal behind the wheel. One Eight said that he never drove
fast because he had too much respect for his life and safety. He
added, however, that there are certain stop signs that he ignores
because they are in the wrong location. "They shouldn't have put
those stop signs there. They should have put them to stop cars
going the other way. It must have been a political deal."

One man described driving with his father:

*We were speeding along when suddenly we swerved into the next
lane and cut off another driver. I said, "Dad, you cut that guy off." He
looked at me, glared, and snarled, "He's got brakes, don't he? That's
what he's got brakes for."*

The Mafia don is an Eight role in our society, as the Yakuza are
in Japan. He has a strong moral code. He will never kill you in
your mother's house. He protects and takes care of the family, protects the community, makes the community a safe place, and takes
care of the kids. If you have a problem, he'll give you some money.
The don's position is taking care of the family as the underdog in
a hostile world. All he asks in return is to kiss his ring and have
respect.

Since society is the enemy with unfair advantages built into its
system, society's rules do not apply to the Eight.

Talking Style: Laying Trips

The talking style is called *laying trips*. Nines tell you endless sagas,
while Eights say, "The trouble with you is . . ." Their humor can
be sadistic and provocative. Eights feel obliged to tell you what
you should and shouldn't be doing. They feel it is their duty to let
you know what's good for you and what's wrong with you. They
may enjoy putting you down and making you feel uncomfortable.

When entering a new situation, Eights will quickly size it up, determine who the leader is, and challenge him for position.

Eights have a sense of self-righteousness, contrasted with the moral rectitude of Ones. When an Eight lays a trip on you, it is coming from a sense of superiority and competence, as well as a physical compulsion within the body to take a dominant position. A self-employed seminar leader shares her experience of her aggressive style, which others often take personally:

I'm hard to work for. I've had secretaries who quit on me because I'll come in and say, "Is that all you've done?!" Because I know that I could do it twice as well and twice as fast. Now when I hire someone, I give them permission to call me on it and call me on the tone of voice. I can say that over the years I've gotten much less defensive about getting critical feedback. I get so much of it! People misinterpret my intensity for anger. Like the way I am speaking right now, they misinterpret THIS for anger. But I'm not angry; I'm just intense.

I was thrown out of a spiritual group that I'd been in for thirteen years because they just didn't like my energy. Wherever I go people tell me I interrupt them; my voice isn't right. I'm always hurting people and I never mean to. The truth just comes out, and it always astonishes me.

The Trap: Justice

The trap of Eight is *justice*. Because they were mistreated as children, Eights become champions of the underdog. They will stand up and fight the system in the name of justice. They are capable of overthrowing the government in the name of justice. While Eights often do good work for the cause of the underdog, the self-righteous strokes of this service feed the fixation, often putting them more deeply to sleep.

Danton, a classic film of the French Revolution stars Gerard Depardieu, a hedonist Sexual Eight playing Danton, of the same fixation. Robespierre is brilliantly portrayed as a One fixation and the duel between them, ending with Danton at the guillotine, offers a deep meditation on the two competing fixations, both certain that they are right. Danton goes to his death at the guillotine because of his overconfident certainty that since he is right in fighting for justice, he is in control, and no jury would ever convict him.

The trap door here is when Eights are willing to give their lives for justice. In this willingness, there is a possibility of the old life burning up and the discovery of truth beyond justice. Oskar Schindler, a Sexual Eight, is a shining example of this. A Nazi collaborator, womanizer, war profiteer, and alcoholic, Schindler risked his life and lost his fortune to save his Jewish workers from the Nazi death camps. This is a wonderful example of how the basic goodness of the heart can motivate the fixation into acts of ego-transcendence.

Defense Mechanism: Denial

The defense mechanism in the Eight is *denial*. Denial works in two ways. The first is to deny any guilt and project the blame onto someone else. The second form of denial is when an Eight is feeling strong emotions and is unaware of the feelings. Emotions are often denied because they are considered a sign of weakness, vulnerability, or guilt.

In Eights, denial comes from having been inconsistently punished as children and feeling the need to defend themselves against a hostile world. The Eight is a tender, sweet, frightened child who has put on a hard warrior mask. The stance of appearing competent, and the denial of emotions or wrongdoing, are both strategies for dealing with terror and rage.

In relationship, when confronted by the partner about what they are really feeling, the Eight tendency is to deny that they are feeling anything. While the partner can be aware of the hostile behavior and the feelings of rage, the Eight denies anything is wrong and blames the partner for finding fault.

One evening a man reported about his return to a group, as it re-assembled after a break:

I run upstairs, I don't walk upstairs, I run upstairs. I had just come back from dinner and I passed this lady and I bumped her purse. My first thought was, 'What's she doin' with a big fuckin' purse like that?' There was no thought like, 'Hey, maybe I'm a little pushy here.' It wasn't that, it's instant blame. It's always just boom. It's instantaneous. It's quicker than thought, almost.

Avoidance: Weakness

The avoidance is *weakness*. Eights always appear to be competent in order to avoid weakness. You know they are working on themselves when they allow themselves to appear tender in social or work situations.

The Eight's stance is: "I'm competent. I am not weak. I can handle it." It is usually only after considerable work on themselves that Eights are willing to be vulnerable and surrender to the moment instead of dominating it. Avoiding weakness plays into the defense mechanism of denial. The vulnerable, tender emotions are denied or overlooked in the mask of toughness.

One Eight, after working on himself, reported:

Innocence is something I had never experienced. Now that I have tasted it, it is all that I want. But people don't allow you to be innocent. They expect something else. So I've put rage out there and found that to be much more acceptable.

Ty Cobb, the great Hall of Fame baseball player, bragged to his biographer, Al Stump, that he had killed a man in Detroit in 1912. Three thugs armed with a knife assaulted him on his way to catch a train to a ballgame. He was carrying a pistol with a raised sight at the end of the barrel. When the gun failed to fire, the assailants cut him in the back. He began pummeling them with his fists so furiously that they finally fled. Cobb, instead of feeling relief at his escape, ran after them, pursuing one into a dead-end alley.

"I used that gun sight to rip and slash and tear him for about ten minutes until he had no face left," Cobb told the interviewer. "I left him there, not breathing, in his own rotten blood."

Cobb wrapped a makeshift bandage over his wound, caught the train to the game, and got a double and a triple. After the game, he was treated for the five-inch knife wound in his back.

The Dichotomy: Puritan/Hedonist

The dichotomy is called *puritan/ hedonist*. This dichotomy reflects different styles of expressing excess. As in all of the fixations, both poles of the polarity are present.

To everyone who knows them, puritan Eights appear maniacally obsessive about work. Working longer and harder and getting up earlier is a badge of excessiveness that the puritan Eight sometimes uses to gain leverage in relationships. Handling many tasks simultaneously, puritan Eights are always pushing against the constraints of time. After work, they may drink hard and play hard, appearing hedonistic to anyone not of the Eight fixation.

The style of the hedonist Eight is bragging. Not bragging about how hard they are working, but about how late they stayed out last night and how hard they partied. One man reported that while in jail in the early 1960s, a survey was taken as to the favorite role models of the inmates. The first-place winner and unanimous choice was Dean Martin, because he always had a drink in one hand, a beautiful woman on the other, lots of money, and a couch behind him.

Like all the fixations, Eights embody both poles of the dichotomy all the time, but one style is predominantly presented to the world. Whichever style is used, Eights will use it to dominate, avoid emotional vulnerability, and prove that they are superior.

A good example of this polarity is a pair of country cousins, Jerry Lee Lewis and Jimmy Swaggart. After growing up and raising hell together as teenagers, Jerry Lee Lewis went on to a career as a wild hedonistic rock 'n roller who did prison time for marrying his underage cousin. Jimmy Swaggart went on to a puritan career as a TV evangelist, with a holier-than-thou attack on sinners, until he was brought down for picking up prostitutes while cruising in his car.

Or consider the difference between the puritan Hillary Clinton and the hedonist Bette Midler; or between Michelle Obama and Mae West.

Subtypes

Preservation: Satisfactory Survival

When the passion of lust runs on the Self-preservation instinct, it is called *satisfactory survival*. If the basic survival needs are covered, the Self-preservation Eight feels good. The place of hardcore survivalists, these people enjoy living outside of society's conventions. They take pleasure in knowing that they don't need anyone else to survive. The Aryan Brotherhood, who live by trapping and hunting in northern Idaho, is most likely peopled with Self-preservation Eights.

An Eight who was making good money as a waiter in the 1960s was living in a cardboard fort in a friend's backyard. He lived that way for two years. He ran an extension cord out from the house so he could watch TV; he was warm, he had all the basics, and he truly enjoyed it.

I described him in a workshop and another Self-preservation Eight said, "You know, it wasn't a fort, but I lived in a plywood shack in somebody's backyard and we were allowed to use electricity only to shave." As he told us this story, he puffed up with pleasure and filled the room with his energy while he laughed at his own jokes. He said he loved living this way because he was beating the system. He was getting away with something, and it was both fun and good enough. Other Eights I know have lived in tree houses, cars, and garages. Another Eight recounted that the only cars he liked were big, old Cadillacs because they were such a comfortable ride, and you could sleep right in the back.

Self-preservation Eights are often crustier, more grizzled, or pricklier, more like a badger than other Eights. Since they don't need anyone else to survive, they put less attention on socialization skills.

Roseanne Barr is a good example of a hedonist Self-preservation Eight.

Another Self-Preservation hedonist Eight woman reported:

When trying to get a man I'm usually jealous of Twos, because they can do that, and I can't. [imitates a coy Two] I'd love to rope them in [laughter]. My pride also makes sure nobody sees that actually. I've even considered maybe I should tell all my friends I've become a hermit? But then I think, "What about my dinner parties?" [laughter] You know, it's like [laughs] I won't have anybody to party with. That's not an option. [laughter] I knew I was sensitive in this way. I work alone, I live alone, all that I can do to just make sure that I don't have to run into people who tell me what to do and say, "you know what your problem is . . . "I should wear a t-shirt which first says, "Don't Fix Me. Not Fixable." And "Beware of the Dog."

Lee Marvin, George C. Scott, and Broderick Crawford are male examples of Self-preservation Eights.

Social: Friendship

When lust uses the Social instinct, it is called *friendship*. Loyalty to friends, and sometimes gangs becomes one of the major themes in life. Once you get on the Social Eight's friend list, you will be there for life, unless you engage in betrayal.

Social Eights are often willing to work it out with their friends, always wanting to confront in order to stay clear. As a rule, Social subtypes enjoy groups of friends together at the same time. Rarely does the Sexual subtype organize a lunch outing with half a dozen friends. A Social Eight told us that playing a pickup game of basketball was better than sex. For the Social Eight, there is a real loyalty to friends, which lasts until death.

A young woman I know reported that whenever she returned home from college, she would always visit her friends first, then her boyfriend, and then family. When she broke up with her high school sweetheart, she insisted on keeping him as a best friend. As a Nine, he didn't understand it, but he went along. Years later when she married, the old high school sweetheart was there celebrating.

Michelle Obama demonstrates the characteristics of the puritan Social Eight. As a Social Eight, rather than the possessive, guarding, and consuming of the family that we see in Donald Trump, the Sexual subtype, Michelle is the family. The family flows from her as the source, power, and direction. It is her identity as she nourishes it and guides it.

The sexual Eight shows up differently. A Mafia don who is a Sexual Eight is loyal to his people, but he may not be friends with any of them, not even his mistresses.

Sexual: Possession/Surrender

While all Sexual subtypes seem to prefer one-on-one relationships, the Eight carries it to the extreme by wanting to possess the beloved. Issues also arise around being able to surrender to the beloved. This doesn't necessarily mean that Eights require monogamy or experience intense jealousy. One sexual Eight I know referred to his open relationship:

The reason it's okay for my partner to have other lovers is that I feel we are so totally bonded, it's safe for her to have other lovers. I believe there is nobody else who could ever take my place.

Possession/surrender really has to do with possessing the beloved totally, and then being able to surrender as well. Who's on top becomes an issue that the Eight uses to avoid opening to the tender vulnerable feelings of intimacy and loss of control.

A male Sexual Eight reported having had a love affair with a female Sexual Eight:

There were issues about who was on top on every level of our rela-tionship from money to food to sex. She was always "doing" for me. She would buy me flowers. I've never had anybody court me and buy me flowers, candy, or gifts.

I realized my own patterns and that the seduction of the Sexual Eight has to do with possessing the beloved. I had never realized that giving a gift is a way of possessing. Until it was happening to me, I never realized the level of aggression and control that manifest in ostensibly taking care of somebody. It was a complete surprise.

Additional Exemplars

Oprah is a puritan Sexual Eight. Her charisma, like Trump's, like all Sexual Eights, can fill a room, regardless of size. (It was Gurdjieff who called this a leaking of sexual energy through the eyes). It is a form of sexual plumage. She is an example of the genuine desire to serve, which is a force deeper than fixation, expressing through fixation. In any case, there is never a question of who is the boss.

Unevolved Eights typify the chauvinist macho position in soci-ety, exemplified by movie roles that Lee Marvin, Robert Mitchum, Sean Penn, and Al Pacino usually play. The characters always have a threatening quality right below the surface. They are always dan-gerous and excessive: Samuel L. Jackson in *Chiraq* displaying the hedonist, and in *Pulp Fiction*, the puritan hit man, shows his range as an actor as long as he is playing Eights. Laurence Fishburne in Othello is a brilliant examination of the puritan Sexual Eight.

Robert De Niro, playing a championship boxer in *Raging Bull*, is a classic example of the raging Self-preservation hedonist Eight. In *This Boy's Life*, De Niro shows a more complex version of the Eight personality. At the end of the movie, the character is left scream-ing in the street, "What about me?!" This is the classic cry of self-ishness, but expressed by the Eight as an angry scream of rage.

An unevolved Eight is the personification of the antisocial personality, as well as the bully and the bigot. Archie Bunker is a caricature of the Eight personality. Sheriff Jim Clark, an Eight, was famous for his beatings of black civil rights protesters in Selma, Alabama in the 1960s. Huey Newton and the Black Panthers are also Eights.

Jack Nicholson, an Eight, plays Eights in all of his movies. Some of his classic portrayals include:

- A small-time con, a social Eight, who tries to beat the system while giving his life to stick up for the underdog in the classic Ken Kesey story, *One Flew Over the Cuckoo's Nest.*

- The teamster leader Jimmy Hoffa, a Self-preservation Eight, in *Hoffa;*

- An army general in *A Few Good Men;* and

- The Devil, a Sexual Eight, in *The Witches of Eastwick.*

Out driving one day, Jack Nicholson became annoyed with the way the driver in front of him was driving. In a rage, he bolted out of the car and with his golf club in hand, began beating the car of the unsuspecting driver.

A lot of actors may play Eights, but you can easily tell the difference. Steve McQueen, a Six, played Eights; Marlon Brando, a Four, usually played Eights as a boxer, dock worker, motorcycle outlaw, and Emilio Zapata, but there was always a sadness and often a lament as part of the role. His, *"I could have been a contender,"* from the film *On the Waterfront,* was one of the great lines of all time.

Clint Eastwood, a One, played Eights in his early roles, from spaghetti Westerns to cops. If you examine the energy that these actors manifest as they play these roles, the contrast to a genuine Eight like Jack Nicholson becomes immediately apparent.

Ike Turner, of the former Ike and Tina Turner Review, was a hedonist Sexual Eight. In an interview he stated that yes, he did occasionally hit his women, "but only when they deserved it!" He told the interviewer, "I don't regret nothing I've ever done, abso-lutely nothing, man, because it took all of that to make me what I am — and I love me today . . . . Yeah, I hit her [Tina], but I didn't hit her more than the average guy beats his wife."

During the interview, Turner fondled his female companion and bragged about his sexual conquests. "I started balling when I was six years old. I started getting married when I was fourteen. I've been married ten times."

Growing up in Mississippi during the Depression, Turner, the son of a preacher and a seamstress, began working at the age of six. At eight, he was selling scrap iron, doing hustles and other odd jobs. He ran away to Memphis briefly and received a thrashing from his mother for it. Still, he continued to skip school and hang out at a pool hall, where he first discovered music. He flouted the law, used drugs heavily, and when he was flush with money, left bowls of cocaine all over his hotel rooms so friends could indulge themselves.

Chogyam Trungpa, an Oxford-educated Tibetan Lama, dedi-cated his life to the service of humanity. His books are brilliant in their crystalline luminosity. Naropa Institute, which he founded, was in the vanguard of creating a new cultural consciousness, as is his Shambhala Training. Known to fall down drunk on his way to the podium to deliver a brilliant speech, he did nothing to hide either his drinking or his womanizing, once taking the wife of a devotee into the bedroom while the devotee sat outside. Trungpa died at forty-six from complications arising from excessive con-sumption of liquor.

Fritz Perls, the father of Gestalt therapy, made his living teach-ing the expression of anger. Fritz loved to call his clients and students on any "bullshit." At a twenty-year reunion of Gestalt therapists, all trained by Fritz, issues that had been suppressed for twenty years began to surface. The women felt sexually abused by Fritz and talked about his tendency to come on to women of all ages, shapes, and sizes. The men, on the other hand, expressed feelings of being put down and emasculated.

Fritz was perceived as the genius father with complete power. Apparently, no one ever had enough power in any situation to challenge him. Fritz, as is true of all Eights to varying degrees, was a master of maintaining control and the upper hand by appearing competent.

As Fritz Perls lay dying in a hospital in Canada, his last words were an attempt to maintain control. Told that he must stay in bed and use a bedpan instead of going to the bathroom, Perls lifted himself out of bed and on his way to the toilet said, "No one tells me what to do." Those were his last words as he keeled over dead.

It has been difficult for women to be Eights in our society, although that may be changing now. Domination and anger are considered male roles, so in the past when women manifested power and competence, they were often shunned by society. Some female Eights go underground and play passive, sweet roles on the surface, while acting out their lust behind the scenes. Yet, there are a lot of powerful female Eights:

- Oprah, is a puritan Sexual eight.

- Madame Blavatsky, the cigar-smoking queen of Theosophy, was a Self-preservation Eight.

- Gertrude Stein and Mother Jones were probably Eights.

- Michelle Obama, Hillary Clinton, and Katharine Hepburn are examples of puritan Social Eights.

Exemplars by Subtype

Self-Preservation~Satisfactory Survival:

These are the crustiest, growliest of the Eights. Since they don't need anyone else to survive, they have not polished their people skills.

*Slobodan Milosevic, Jack Nicholson, Harvey Keitel, Fritz Perls,
Roseanne Barr, George C. Scott, Golda Meir, Jimmy Hoffa, Ethel
Merman, Ty Cobb, Broderick Crawford, Quentin Tarantino, Waylon
Jennings, Ernest Borgnine, Ann Sothern, Bella Abzug, Moms Mabley,
Josef Stalin, Madame Blavatsky, Poland*

Social~Friendship:

These are the people who have best friends for life, and are always
in a tight family and/or social circle.

*Michelle Obama, Hillary Clinton, Laura Dern, Edie Falco, Judy
Davis, Robert De Niro, Keith Richards, Lyndon Johnson, Lucille Ball,
Hank Williams, Charles Bronson, Robert Duvall, Richard Harris, Lucky
Luciano, Katharine Hepburn, Billy Martin, Danny DeVito, Audrey
Meadows, Spiro Agnew, Sea Shepard, Ireland*

Sexual~Possession/Surrender:

These Eights are the most confident of themselves and their sexuality. The lust leaks through the eyes.

*Bill Clinton, Samuel L. Jackson, Serena Williams, Al Pacino, James
Gandolfini (Tony Soprano), Russell Crowe, Sean Connery, Liam Neeson,
Javier Bardem, Saddam Hussein, Susan Sarandon, Danny Glover,
Laurence Fishburne, Richard Burton, Oskar Schindler, Mohammar
Khadafi, Idi Amin, Mae West, Frank Sinatra, Jimmy Swaggart, Anne
Bancroft, Yul Brynner, Bessie Smith, Huey Newton, Anthony Quinn,
Zorba the Greek, Gerard Depardieu, Mike Tyson, Chogyam Trungpa,
George Gurdjieff, the Maori of New Zealand, gangsta rap and Israel*

Point One: The Interiorized Anger Point

Essence:	Purity
Holy idea:	Perfection
Holy path:	Serenity
Chief feature:	Resentment
Passion:	Anger
Idealization:	"I am righteous."
Talking style:	Preaching
Trap:	Perfection
Defense mechanism:	Reaction formation
Avoidance:	Anger
Dichotomy:	Rigid / Sensitive
Subtypes:	Self-preservation~Worry Social~Inadaptability Sexual~Jealousy

The Drive to Perfection

The interiorized version of Nine is One, a very interesting anger point since both the passion and the avoidance are anger. This is the only point on the Enneagram where the passion and the avoidance are the same. In a sense, these are people driving through life with the brakes on.

The fixation for the One is centered around the anal muscles. People with these fixations can be the archetype for the word "uptight." Anal-retentiveness manifests as a need for tight control and being right.

Where Nines have lost the personal position, and Eights have a strong personal position on everything, Ones want the right position and therefore struggle to do the right thing. Quite often in Ones you see the furrowed brows, the thin lips of anger, and the moral superiority exhibited by the famous painting, *American Gothic*.

While Eights are the bad boys and girls, Ones are the good boys and girls. Even though the One fixation is an anger point, a One will seldom get angry like an Eight. If they do explode in anger, they discuss it with themselves afterwards, judging the appropriateness of their action. This is the home of the judge. Every fixation has a super-ego, but for the One it is the judge judging the judge.

The One's driving rage for perfection is fueled by the terror of being wrong. In order to be right, you have to know what is correct in any given moment. Not knowing is terrifying, and therefore avoided by means of concepts, beliefs, sermons, or peculiar nostrums. Ones are always improving themselves.

Ones appear to be perfect at whatever they do. I have a friend with a One fixation who lived in a rustic cabin in Oregon. She appeared to be the perfect mother and the perfect wife. She was living in a home with no electricity or running water. She and her husband cut wood for their heat. They had no money. But when you visited their home, everything was exactly perfect and in its place. There was fresh bread baking in the oven, little gingham curtains pulled back off the window, and local wildflowers were artfully arranged in colored bottle vases. Everything had been swept and was spotless. You could eat off the floors. It looked perfect.

The perfectionist personality manifests in whatever the One places a high value on, and this can vary considerably from person to person. It would be tempting to assume that the perfectionist personality manifests in every arena of their life, but this is often not the case. In the words of a One,

My house is often messy, and I am not the most organized person, but when it comes to doing something I place a high value on, I go the extra mile to make it right.

Another One, who keeps her house immaculately clean and orderly, reports that her office at work is relatively messy. She places a high value on the appearance of her home, but not the appearance of her office. She just keeps it organized enough so that she can do her job well.

However well they appear to the rest of us, Ones feel that they are never quite good enough. This is because they are always comparing themselves to an ideal standard. Striving for improvement is a One imperative. Here a workshop participant speaks of having the need for perfection while growing up:

I had to be perfect, but I never saw myself as perfect. I always saw myself as never making it as much as I wanted to. I was good at everything no matter what I did. I was really good, except that it just wasn't good enough. It wasn't what I wanted to be.

When I had my own children, boy, did they have to do their homework right! In fact, I almost ended up doing it for them, because I wanted their homework to be really perfect. This was until the teachers realized that their homework was so perfect that it couldn't be theirs. I was asked to leave them alone, and let them learn from their own mistakes. After that, I felt a lot better. I felt a big weight lift off my shoulders.

Ones are often found to be doctors, small business owners, and self-employed professionals. Brain surgery, where precise control is mandatory, can be a One profession. It can be very hard for them to work in a bureaucracy because they have a sense of inadaptability, a strong moral code, and a willingness to fight for what they believe is right.

Reformers

Ones can be sermonizing preachers, like Billy Graham and Jerry Falwell, as well as social reformers like Mahatma Gandhi, Martin Luther King, and Ralph Nader. One is the place of utopian thinking.

Napoleon, a Social One, was exiled onto Elba. His first move was to reform the government there. He instituted changes in the tax laws, ushered in democratic elections and then started making the small militia into a proper military force. He built a sewage system, roads, and reformed the education system along the way.

Ones are very free thinkers, not at all swayed by popular opinion, and usually with a utopian fantasy somewhere in the back of their minds. This is an expression of the idealism of the Seven, which is the core point that the One is wrapped around. (The movement of the points is discussed in a later chapter.)

Usually the belief is that if everyone would just pull themselves up by their own bootstraps, we'd all do fine. Mary Baker Eddy, the founder of Christian Science and its belief in the healing power of the mind, is a classic example of a One.

Anger

Anger manifests first as a sensation in the body. This is a body thought. Ones will get angry and then blame themselves. They don't know how to express anger appropriately. Penance, in the Catholic tradition of people punishing themselves for being bad, is a One concept. Wearing a hair shirt is also a very One-ish action. For the One, being angry is not acceptable because it means a loss of control. Often anger cannot be expressed publicly, for it would be impolite. Anger would also mean that Ones are judgmental and therefore not perfect. This also makes them angry. Unless the One finds that rare moment when they know their anger is completely justifiable, they are likely to feel that they are wrong for feeling anger and will attempt to manage it, control it, or repress it.

My experience with anger is that I get indigestion a lot. I contain it. I get angry when I don't feel that my efforts are appreciated; when I compromise myself by doing what I think I should do, but don't want to do; and when I perceive that others are not being straight with me. In relationship, when something comes up that makes me feel angry, I can feel the rage in the moment, but I have a hard time justifying it, so then I try to talk myself out of it. I usually decide that I'm not going to talk about it with the person, because it is my problem, and I have to deal with it. I will then feel the need to do something physical while I talk to myself to try to get rid of the anger. I usually carry it for a while, and later it may leak out as sarcastic remarks and criticalness. I used to be able to carry the anger for a long time, but fortunately, I don't hold on to it as long anymore. I am discovering that I can choose to make space for things that used to make me angry, and when things come up, I can just let them go.

Time, dirt, and money

All the obsessive-compulsives have issues around time, dirt, and money. Eights can be habitually late, sloppy with food stains on their clothes, and a roll of hundreds in their front pockets. One Eight reports that he doesn't wear clothes but food magnets: *If something spills anywhere some of it will land on my shirt.*

On the other hand, cleanliness for Ones is a very strong issue as well as wearing their clothes as a uniform, like George Washington. Usually they are extremely clean, scrubbing rather than just tidying. Obsessive hand washing is an example of the obsessive compulsive impulse, coupled with the defense mechanism of reaction formation.

When traveling through Switzerland, a One culture, I noticed that the floor of the airport in Zurich was cleaner than the kitchen in many homes in the United States, unless, of course, it is the kitchen of a One. A female One who is very particular about the cleanliness of the floors in her home shared the following:

For me, keeping the floor clean is very symbolic of the futility of the obsessiveness in my behavior. I have this image of a perfect floor, and I try to keep the floor clean to satisfy this image, but it is impossible. When someone tracks in dirt or drops some crumbs, which I will certainly see, it is like an assault on the order in my world. Although it is impossible, I am obsessed with keeping it totally clean. I actually really enjoy sweeping and scrubbing the floor. This gives me a sense of control and order and a great sense of satisfaction.

Part of the reason I feel this obsessiveness with the floor is that in order for me not to focus on seeing the dirt that is there, I have to relinquish control, and if I give up control, it feels like I can't think, and everything is descending into chaos. In cleaning, which feels like nesting, I am creating order, which gives me a sense of security. Then, I feel that things are predictable and there are no surprises. I feel padded from fear of the unknown.

Another part of the reason for this behavior is that I want to be the "good girl" and be praised for doing what is right, which is to keep order. I want the work that I have done to be recognized and appreciated. If you get dirt or crumbs on my floor, what it means to me is that you are being selfish and lazy and don't appreciate what I have done.

The Super Ego

Just as Eight is the home of the blamer, One is the home of the super-ego, or internalized judgment of one's own imperfection. While every ego has a super-ego, or judge, for the One this is especially strong, like a double dose. Here a female One describes what this is like:

You have to be very vigilant in finding out what is the right thing to do, because you have this judge in your head, which is like a higher self. And if you don't do the right thing this judge says, "You should have done it this way. Oh, why didn't you . . . ?" This judge is very critical, so it is mandatory that you find the right way to do it. In order to do that, you have to really do some research, and very carefully discover what is right so that this sense of this judge in your head won't beat you up.

That aspect of me seems like this morally right person or God, some-one that is going to keep me on the straight and narrow. When I look back on being a teenager, I was very moral. I never did anything wrong. I was always too afraid to do anything wrong.

James Madison gives us a One perspective in the Federalist Paper 51:

If men were angels, no government would be necessary. In framing a government which is to be administered by men over men, the great difficulty lies in this: You must first enable the government to control the governed; and in the next place, to control itself.

Anger can leak out in sarcastic remarks. It makes the One hyper-critical and self-critical. It also creates passive-aggressive behavior. Ones often have very fine posture, thin lips, and furrowed brows. The features on the One's face are often quite symmetrical. People sometimes feel that Ones are looking down their noses at them.

Dichotomy

George Bernard Shaw had a classic One face, very thin-lipped, with judgmental eyes looking out from under his brow. He was a champion of women's rights long before it was popular. His play, *Pygmalion*, made into the show, *My Fair Lady*, is a comedy about taking a guttersnipe and passing her off at the ball. This represents a One's sarcastic view of "polite society," as well as their dichotomy of seeing women as either whores or virgins. Along with real respect, male Ones often harbor a lot of hostility toward women. In this Jekyll/Hyde personality, there are dichotomies in every-thing. Consider Bill Cosby here.

There is a strong libido, a secret garden of sexuality, that is somewhat shielded from the harsh super-ego. A One may be wild in the bedroom and hate public displays of affection. There is a portrait of a One in a Polish film called *Bitter Harvest*. The protago-nist is a priest who gave up the priesthood and became a farmer in World War II. The film revolves around his hiding a Jewish woman in the basement of his farmhouse during the Nazi occupation. He does it because it is the morally correct thing to do. However, there is a sexual dimension represented by having this Jewish woman in his basement. On the one hand, he wants to be moral, upright, and protect her. On the other hand, he is lusting after her. He gets drunk, climbs into the basement to sexually assault her, and forgets about it in the morning. (One of my early Enneagram teachers, Kathleen Speeth, once remarked that, "The super-ego of the One is highly soluble in alcohol.")

Upon hearing this, one person reported that in all of his wedding pictures, he and his bride are both sitting and solemnly addressing the camera. It is rare to even have a photo of them holding hands, let alone kissing, but they made love in the church before the wedding.

Spanking and kinky sex can be a way that sexuality gets twisted in the One fixation. English judges dressing as schoolboys to be spanked by the dominatrix is a One phenomenon. John Cleese, a Social One, in *Fawlty Towers* is hilarious spanking himself as a naughty boy and is well worth watching on YouTube.

Suppression of anger

Creativity and sexuality are also tied to anger. When Ones accept that it is okay to feel and express anger, creativity and sexuality come up as well. As long as the anger is suppressed, there can be trouble with sexual energy and creativity. Quite often illness is related to suppressed anger; this can manifest as a tightness in the intestinal tract. Lenin and Napoleon, both Social Ones, suffered from digestive issues, with Napoleon dying from intestinal cancer.

Ones usually exhibit a very tight musculature. A woman married to a One said it took her husband two years to get into a half lotus, and he worked on it every day. The point here is not only the tightness, but also that he worked on it every day. John Cleese uses his rigid One body for physical comedy as he goose-steps on the same TV series.

Society and Culture

Switzerland's Cantons, with their respect for the small farmer and citizen democracy, are examples of One culture. In all One cultures there is a clean, prim, prudish exterior, along with hidden red-light districts and an idealized respect for free thinking.

I once met a One who worked for Sandoz Pharmaceuticals in Switzerland. I was very curious about how he could deal with having a bureaucracy and bosses over him. He said it wasn't a problem, because at Sandoz there were no bosses. Everyone worked in a team of quality circles. This is a natural strategy for a corporation in a One culture, like Switzerland, to adopt.

Amsterdam, a social One culture, has a tolerance for marijuana and counterculture lifestyle. This is not because the local population supports drugs, which in fact the majority does not, but because they support free thinking and a person's right to live the way she wishes.

The United States was a One country when it was first settled. The Puritans exemplify the One style, as do the Amish. A puritan work ethic and a Calvinistic point of view are One positions. George Washington, the solemn, rigid, upright General with a stone face and a perfect uniform is the Father of our Country

Passion/Avoidance: Anger

One is both the most dichotomized and the most polarized of all the fixations. Both the passion and the avoidance are anger; both the trap and the holy idea are *perfection.*

Ones have an idealized vision of how things could be perfect. They notice imperfection and become resentful. This resentment can slip out as biting, sarcastic humor. Ones are always a little angry. The anger leaks out in hyper-criticality and often manifests in muscular tension. Ones are the most critical of themselves. This may be the most self-punishing point on the Enneagram.

While a Nine feels anger and goes unconscious, and an Eight feels anger and expresses it as rage, a One feels anger and attempts to avoid it. Because of this duality, the super-ego processes the anger as the One decides whether it is correct to feel angry or not. The super-ego is the judge. The judge decides on the appropriateness of anger and all other behaviors, thoughts, and feelings.

When anger arises in the body, if the super-ego decides it is not proper to be angry in the moment, rather than expressing the anger, the One holds onto it and becomes resentful. The anger leaks out as the One notices imperfection and becomes sarcastic. The pressure of the suppression of the anger leads to trouble with muscular tension, headaches, orthopedic problems, joint problems, arthritis, and colitis.

Childhood Setting

As children, Ones often report being punished appropriately and consistently. They were punished for things they did that were bad and rewarded for things they did that were good. Ones believe that if you do the right thing, you are rewarded, and if you do a bad thing, you are punished.

The One's anger is held in the body anally. When Ones were children, they lost the battle of potty training. Quite often the unconscious, unexpressed rage over potty training is at the core of this fixation's issues of control.

In working with Ones therapeutically, I have inevitably discovered that there is tension in the musculature around the anus. This is the place where tension first begins in the body. It can also manifest in tightness in the jaw, as with Clint Eastwood, and in tight musculature in general.

A male Sexual One spoke about his childhood and the crystallization of the fixation:

When I was about three years old I was down by the pond outside of our house. I was fascinated with all the life there. I would sit and watch it for hours. One day I saw frogs making love. I became quite excited and ran in to tell my mother. My mother was playing cards with her girlfriends when I came in and said, "Mama, I just saw the two-backed frogs!" They all laughed at me. I became terribly ashamed and rushed into my room. I knew then that I would never put myself in a potentially humiliating circumstance again.

A female One reported:

When I was a little girl, just out of diapers, my older sisters were playing with me. We were playing on the bed and they put diapers on me. Then they took the diapers off and told me to pee. At that moment, my father burst into the room. I remember standing on the bed naked, crying, "I didn't do it! I didn't do it!"

She now has a position as a moral crusader.

Idealization: "I am righteous."

The idealization is, "I am righteous." There is an idealized view of perfection that manifests as a strong, internalized moral code.

The classic One historical period was Victorian England, where skirts were used to hide chair and sofa legs. This was also a time when the best pornography in the English language was written. Ones are often the censors who watch dirty movies all day to decide what is proper and appropriate for the general public.

Milton Erickson, the famous psychiatric hypnotist, saw his clients' hair as a reflection of their sexual self-image. Erickson believed the grooming and parting of hair was symbolic of how his patients considered their genitals. Ones most always have neat hair; often they have "helmet haircuts." There is the sense that they could ride in the back of a pickup truck and no part of their hair would ever be mussed. Britain's former Prime Minister,

Margaret Thatcher, Prince Charles, and Dianne Feinstein are also good examples of this. They have hairdos that look as if they would break if they ever fell down.

Talking Style: Preaching

The talking style is called *preaching*. This can take the form of a sermon from a pulpit or a lecture on how you could be more perfect as a mate or child. The tone of sermonizing can come through a sense of superior morality, and may be considered condescending.

The Trap: Perfection

For the One, the perceived need for *perfection* manifests as a desire for mastery over untamed nature. As a style, Ones tend to think that a well-tended farm is more beautiful than a stand of trees. Ones often live in houses with lawns that are almost militaristically neat. There is never any lush overgrowth; it has all been neatly trimmed, and possibly put into geometric shapes.

As a trap, perfection is the rationale for attempting to control the world. It is the desire to tame nature in order to make it perfect. Ones often describe walking into a room and immediately noticing what is wrong. One person pointed out that the electric outlet at the baseboard of the room where we were meeting was slightly askew. This person noticed slight smudges and some wrinkling in the drapes as well. A One doctor I know in New York has a very successful career reading X-rays, looking for the subtle imperfections that allow him to make accurate diagnoses.

The trap of needing to be perfect makes the One angry. After judging themselves as imperfect, they then project this feeling out into the world and become angry about the world's perceived imperfections. Miss Manners and Emily Post were both Ones. This is the place of etiquette, knowing the social rules and then acting properly.

In the following, a One tells a story that is a good description of the trap of perfection. Attention can become fixated on what is wrong, overlooking the experience of actual perfection in the moment:

One Thanksgiving when our family was having a whole bunch of people over to the house, I asked everyone to bring a particular dish. I had asked this one friend to bring a particular kind of vegetable, and I don't remember what kind, but she showed up with brussel sprouts — of all things. I remember I greeted her at the door and she handed me these brussel sprouts, and I was shocked. I thought, "That's not what I asked you to bring." What came up for me was, "Well, how could she do that? No one here likes brussel sprouts."

"Is that what you said to her?" I asked.

No, oh, heavens no! But where the attention moved was to what was wrong. The whole atmosphere for me had changed because my attention moved to what was wrong, even though everything else was so wonderful. All these wonderful people were there, but the attention had moved to that minuscule thing. And the brussel sprouts were really delicious. I loved them!

Given that both the trap and the holy idea are perfection, the possibility for the One is to realize that the appearance of things as they are *is* the perfection, regardless of the One's preconceived notions of how perfection is supposed to look or feel. Surrender to this realization dissolves the rigidity of the One fixation and is the gateway to serenity and love beyond all ideas.

Defense Mechanism: Reaction formation

For the Nine, the defense mechanism is narcotization, using conversation, drugs, food, ideas, etc. For the One, it is *reaction formation*. Reaction formation means that as an impulse comes up from the subconscious, it is changed before reaching consciousness.

My first Enneagram teacher, Jerry Perkins, uses the example of the little boy who is caught masturbating by the priest. The priest says, "Whenever you feel like masturbating, pray." Soon the little boy doesn't feel like masturbating anymore, he just feels like praying. When the urge to masturbate comes up, it gets shifted and comes out into his consciousness as praying.

Another example of reaction formation may occur when a One is terribly overworked. Instead of feeling the need to rest and take a vacation, Ones feel the need to work more. Besides overworking, these people like to plan their lives, and do a lot of scheduling.

Another One said, "Vacation is a big effort for me. I mean, it's really hard to be there and do nothing. I don't like it." Ones usually don't "do nothing." They take scuba diving lessons, or get up at six to play tennis. If they go to a small island, they have to see everything on the island in two days. A One complained because her husband took her on a six-week vacation to Thailand, where they spent days lying on a beach. "It was terrible," she said.

One of the primary characteristics of the One is hating to waste time. Time is obsessively tied to issues of authority and control. Martha Stewart, a Sexual One, on a radio show spoke of her vacations as learning experiences for her children. She detailed the daily activities and full scheduling of the day so as not to waste a precious moment.

The Dichotomy: Rigid/Sensitive

The dichotomy in One is called *rigid/sensitive*. As with all fixations, both poles of this dichotomy are present. Notice how this dichotomy is a version of the Eight dichotomy of puritan/hedonist.

The way this dichotomy reflects itself in the One character is by the One's "stance" in the world. Some Ones appear to be softer and more emotionally sensitive. Other Ones are more militaristic in their bearing, both posturally and emotionally. Al Gore is a rigid One, while Emma Thompson is on the sensitive side of the dichotomy.

Subtypes

Since One and Eight are versions of Nine, the subtypes show the similarities and variations.

The Self-preservation Nine is appetite, or never having enough. The Self-preservation Eight is satisfactory survival. The Self-preservation One is worry about the future.

Notice the variations on a similar theme of attitudes toward survival in the world.

Self-Preservation: Worry

Worry, for the Self-preservation One, is anger projected into the future. This worry is prophylactic, as the Self-preservation One seems to believe that if he can think of everything that can possibly go wrong and worry about it, then he can make plans to avoid future catastrophe.

This is a variation of the magical thinking seen later in point Seven. In Seven, the magical thinking is thinking positively, as in, "If we have good enough thoughts we can fly." In One, the magical thinking is negative: "If I'm worried about all the possible negative consequences, then I can take care of it before it actually happens."

A Self-preservation One said she went to a psychic who told her she was going to live into her nineties. This made her furious because suddenly, she had to worry about her future in a whole different way. "How am I going to take care of myself in my nineties?" She started worrying and then changed her whole life plan. She changed her career as well as her savings plan. When I saw her last she had put all the changes into place but was still worrying prophylactically about the future.

A close acquaintance of mine, a Self-preservation One, was a successful doctor in his mid-forties living in the San Francisco Bay Area. He had a five-year-old daughter and was worried about her future. In order to ensure that her future was taken care of, he moved to the South. He could make more money and live more inexpensively in Tennessee, even though it meant giving up his classes in painting, the one creative outlet he really loved. He has a ten-year plan. After ten or fifteen years, he will have made enough to return to San Francisco, where he really wants to live.

Social: Inadaptability

The Social One is called *inadaptability*. These are the noncon-formist social reformers, such as Robespierre, Lenin, Napoleon, Mahatma Gandhi, Governor Jerry Brown, and Ralph Nader.

These are people willing to take a stand on their moral code. The Social One is also the place of people who either don't want, or refuse to adapt to, the bureaucratic or societal code. These are people often willing to take their moral position to the barricades.

Dr. Kevorkian, a pioneer for legal euthanasia in the US, is a good example of this. Since he was getting away with treating many people who were ready to die with euthanasia, and not be-ing convicted, he had no platform to challenge the law. Because of this, he televised a euthanasia event, thus putting the evidence in the public record so he had to be arrested. He then defended him-self as his own lawyer, ensuring a conviction. In this way, he could now fight for justice, not by practicing as a doctor but by changing the society from a jail cell. In the certainty that they are morally correct, social Ones can take a position and crusade for it.

I've mentioned Robespierre of the French Revolution as a Social One. Robespierre's Terror is the cautionary tale of moral utopian thinking justifying the guillotine. As I mentioned with the Eights, the movie classic, *Danton*, shows the conflict between Robespierre, a One, and Danton, an Eight. You can see how Robespierre's moral rectitude leads to the Reign of Terror. He was not interested in ven-geance and wept over sending his best friend from his early days as a student, Camille DeMoulins, to his death. He begs Camille to repent but ends up doing what he had to do to protect his revolution, having Danton and Camille beheaded.

Robespierre helped to write the most democratic French Constitution of all time, but never implemented it because of his moral certainty that he knew best and first must come brutal repression before freedom. He was an early advocate of eliminating the death penalty, but then enabled the killing of thousands of people in order to try to usher in his moral vision. His belief that the ends justified the means, saying, "You can't have a revolution without a revolution," reappears as Mao's slogan that, "You can't make an omelet without breaking eggs."

V.I. Lenin, of the Russian revolution, was also a Social One who quite literally took his play book from Robespierre. In his moral certainty of how to create a paradise on earth he was willing to first create hell. Like the Jacobins of Robespierre, the Bolsheviks were a fringe minority group willing to use violence to get their way, which was *the right way*. They both used the violence of the mob in service of a dictatorship that ostensibly was to serve "the people." Lenin used Stalin, an Eight, to do the dirty work while Lenin sat in café's with his wife.

Neither Robespierre nor Lenin were personally violent people, and in fact both shunned the viewing of violence. They did not financially gorge themselves on the revolutions that they created, and they both lived rather sedate bourgeois life-styles. But they were willing to order others to do whatever it takes to fulfill the vision, even if it meant wading in blood.

On the other hand, Nelson Mandela is an example of the inadaptability of the One Fixation put into the service of his people instead of a strict moral vision. At some point he agreed with the need of violence in the struggle against the apartheid regime, but never lost his humanity and clarity of service. He ensured there was no retaliation of terror against the old regime.

Gandhi's trading his lawyer suit for a loincloth in his pursuit of freedom for his country through non-violence is another example of the Social One fixation put to good use.

Bernie Sanders, a Social One, has stood firm in his convictions as the only socialist elected to congress since the New Deal. His refusal to compromise and his plan for America have generated true social change. However, his anger, which is his greatest strength is also his Achilles heel. He comes across as angry and preaching and loses support for his program because of the personality that reflects his moral character.

Sexual: Jealousy

When anger leaks into the sexual arena, it manifests as *jealousy*. Jealousy, for the One, is a sense that somebody else may violate our "perfect union."

In the sexual relationship, there's a sense of both perfection and jealousy. You might be at a cocktail party talking with a Sexual One who is an extremely intelligent, bright, evolved person. Suddenly, he psychically gets the vibes and turns to notice his wife talking to someone on the other side of the room. You may notice an automatic response in his expression and tone of voice. The smile gets a little tight and forced, and the voice may rise a bit in pitch. Jealousy and worry that someone else may be violating the union is often an automatic response of the Sexual One.

A male Sexual One reported:

The perfection of the One early on was my hell, because I knew that I couldn't be perfect, so I kind of gave up very early in the game. But the one thing that seemed like would still do the trick, was this mission that I had, and the mission was to spread my seed [laughter] And around that mission I created a whole life. That one simple thing was enough, to create, you know, to create this dancing thing that was called my life.

And I got pretty good at it too. And that's part of the Sexual One is the ease with which I could manipulate the situation so that seduc-

tion was my way. I couldn't ever see a woman as a woman, I only saw a woman as the possible fertile ground for my seed. And the man, of course, was the enemy. And there came a time when I had to face that. And it was . . . "Well without that, who am I? I'm nobody without my dick in my hand," . . . And, of course, I discovered my worse fear, that I was nobody. And that was the greatest discovery.

Additional Exemplars

The founding fathers of the United States are good examples of the One fixation. There is a sense of moral rectitude and purity, as well as freedom of religion and thought. You can think whatever you want. You can also believe anything you want. However, there is a proper way of conducting yourself.

John Lennon, a Self-Preservation One, had the concerned, furrowed brow and thin lips of the One. The proselytizing and preaching in his music reaches its zenith in *Instant Karma*: *"Instant karma's gonna get you. It's got you by the head. Better get yourself together. Pretty soon you're gonna be dead."* He was also very devoted to women's rights. In the last part of his life, he preached about his being a househusband. The antiwar events that he staged by being televised in bed with Yoko Ono is a classic One statement.

Steve Jobs, a Social One, was not an engineer, he was a perfectionist visionary. He was angry and abusive towards his crew, demanding perfection in the look and feel of the Apple. He changed our world, from the iPod to the iPhone with his vision of a connected world, inspired as he said, by his use of LSD while on his spiritual search in India. He stood up to the corporate culture of IBM to make a computer friendly for the rest. He was copied by Bill Gates, a Self-Preservation Three, who set up Microsoft for the mainstream corporate world.

Hugh Hefner was another example of the One fixation in pajamas. The whole Playboy philosophy and image of airbrushed "perfect" women is a very One-ish perspective. Perhaps we all have the image of Hugh Hefner with his pipe, in his robe, shuffling around in his slippers with perfectly neat hair with a playmate on each arm. Playmates are idealized, clean, well-scrubbed girls who are secret hedonists.

In the 1960s, as America emerged from the deadening 1950s, *Playboy* was a pioneer in social nonconformity and took a strong moral stand on freedom of the press, freedom of religion, and freedom of thought. Hefner preached the Playboy philosophy and was always involved in social issues. He was a Midwestern businessman with thin lips, furrowed brow, a look of serious concern, and a lot of tension in his jaw.

Clint Eastwood, another One, generally played Eights in his early movies. Even so, his characterization never came from rage, but rather, from moral superiority. Perhaps his most brilliant role, and the pinnacle of his career, was in *The Unforgiven*, which he also directed. He plays a One gunslinger reformed by his dead wife. He preaches to the kids and works hard slopping the hogs. Out of a desire to give his kids a better life, and because the man he will be paid to kill is described as mutilating women, he once more puts on his guns. But he just doesn't have the heart for killing any-more, until his friend, Morgan Freeman a sweet Nine convinced to come along for the ride, is killed and Eastwood gets drunk. In his drunkenness, the killing rage gets expressed. This is a wonderful movie with a twist — the sheriff, played by Gene Hackman, is an Eight; the outlaw is a One, and the title is perfect. How One-ish can you get beyond *The Unforgiven*?

Another Eastwood-directed film is *Midnight in the Garden of Good and Evil*.

Ayatollah Khomeini governed Iran from a puritanical, fun-damentalist moral position. He was the Plains preacher or the fundamentalist Baptist minister personified.

Prince Charles' nonconformity came out when he supported acupuncture, alternative medicine, and traditional architecture in

England. He is a concerned, solid, moral person with a hairdo that never changes and a secret, kinky sex life.

Colin Kaepernick lost years of his professional football career by standing up for Black Lives Matters by kneeling on one knee and growing his hair.

And finally we have Dr. Bronner's, Liquid Peppermint soap. I recently discovered that Dr. Bronner escaped as a Jew from Germany and was the sole surviving member of the Heilbronner Soap Company, at the time the largest in Germany. Perhaps it was the psychological pain of losing his entire family that drove him a bit mad, but he was still a great soap maker. All the hippies of the sixties who used soap used Dr. Bronner's, or at least they all did on my commune. It could be used for everything from washing the body to washing clothes or dishes. It was free of the chemicals, fragrances and color dyes of commercial soap. But just as importantly perhaps was the label. The labels were filled in tiny script with what we, at the time, called the mad scientist's stoned preaching of Oneness. Reading from the label of a bottle I bought here in Sydney the other day: *Absolute cleanliness is Godliness! Teach the Moral ABC, that unites all mankind free, instantly six billion strong and we are All-ONE.* This is the opening line of a multi-page sermon that spread across every useable space on the label and then changed with the seasons and the fresh batch of soap. But always with the theme of hard work and purification in the service of Oneness.

Exemplars by Subtype

Self-Preservation~Worry:

John Lennon, Margaret Thatcher, Ida Rolf, Bashar al-Assad from Syria, Maggie Smith, Clint Eastwood, Gary Cooper, Lou Gehrig, Mary Baker Eddy, Christian Science, Calvinism, Switzerland

Social~Inadaptability:

Bernie Sanders, Steve Jobs, Adam Driver, Colin Kaepernick, Napoleon, Robespierre, Malcolm X, Nelson Mandela, Leo Tolstoy, Mahatma Gandhi, Buckminster Fuller, Gov. Jerry Brown, A. Solzhenitsyn, Ralph Nader, George Bernard Shaw, Ayatollah Khomeini, Martin Luther, Quakers, the Amish, the Netherlands

Sexual~Jealousy:

Martin Luther King, Leo Tolstoy, Prince Charles, Martha Stewart, Ed Harris, Al Gore, Emma Thompson, Aretha Franklin, Dianne Feinstein, Jean-Luc Picard, Walt Whitman, nudist nature clubs, Sweden

Hysterics: The Image Points

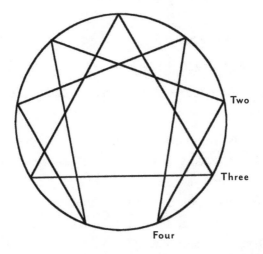

Oh, my soul, turn the heart upside down,
And be absorbed in the Beloved.

– Kabir

In the hysterics, the fixation is crystallized in the emotional body. This is the veiling of love by the search for love from the outside. These are people whose fixations run on emotion. The word "hysteria" is derived from the Greek word for uterus. This syndrome, where the emotions are out of balance, has been projected as a feminine condition. While in Western culture, points Two and Four are perceived as feminine styles, there are, of course, male examples of all the fixations.

The central issue for people in this group is the need for love and approval, along with a perceived inability to be loved for who they are. Self-hatred is the underlying theme for all hysterics. Sometimes called the "relating" group, their style is to move towards people. Central issues revolve around relationship and the question, "Who am I with?"

The different strategies developed by the hysterics center on finding ways to be loved:

- Threes want to be loved for what they produce.

- Twos demand love for being helpful and good caretakers.

- Fours long for love and feel that they should be loved, because they are unique and elite.

Self-esteem is also sought from the outside, so there is always a need for others to reflect back an image. These are not people who will spend their lives alone.

Also called image points, these are people who have sold out their essential being to an image that seems to be required by society. Often the most beautiful people on the Enneagram, the image points have created themselves in the image they have been taught we will love.

Point Three: The Core Image Point

Essence:	Love
Holy Idea:	Compassion
Holy Path:	Veracity
Chief Feature:	Efficiency
Passion:	Deceit
Idealization:	"I am successful"
Talking Style:	Propaganda
Trap:	Efficiency
Defense Mechanism:	Identification
Avoidance:	Failure
Dichotomy:	Overactive/Fantasy
Subtypes:	Self-Preservation~Security Social~Prestige Sexual~Masculine/Feminine

Three is the core hysteric, or image point. These are people who lost touch with their essential being by being seduced by images from the outer world. Just as there appears to be an absence of anger in the core anger point, there appears to be an absence of hysteria in the core hysteric.

Production

Threes gain self-worth through production. Emotions and vital energy are used in the libidinization of product. These people manifest cool competence and maximum efficiency in getting the job done.

Threes were children who very early in life began to believe they could not be loved for themselves, but only for what they produced. Child prodigies, class leaders, overachievers, and head cheerleaders are often the product of this fixation.

A Three describes this motivation to produce in an attempt to earn lovability:

Everything I try to do is an attempt to find out if I am lovable, because always I have these doubts. It feels like a neediness, like I need love. When I was born, the first lesson was, "You are not lovable just for what you are. You have to do things, know things, and have things in order to be lovable." It makes me feel like a dog —"You won't get food unless you perform."

It's difficult to enjoy anything, because there is always a sensation that I have to do something, have something, know something, in order to be acceptable or lovable. If I don't have this, or know that, or do this, nobody's going to love me.

The United States has been a Three culture with image, production, and success as the key values motivating society. Contact with deep emotions is avoided, as the emotional body gets used in production.

A Three spoke of her experience as a cheerleader and homecoming queen. After she won the competition for which she had put out an enormous amount of energy, and was regally smiling and waving as she rode around the stadium, people asked her, "How do you feel about winning?" She told them she felt wonderful, but the truth was, as she revealed years later, that all she had felt inside was a dead emptiness. There were no feelings left, because they had all been put into producing "the homecoming queen" product.

Another woman reported:

I set out to have the most items under my name in the yearbook, so I was in everything. I was homecoming queen and president of my class.

I used to take two sack lunches to school because I was there for both lunch and dinner. At college I did the same thing. I became president of my class. I didn't like the council meetings, and I was not interested in the job, just the title. I remember after I won, walking to the pay phone to call home and thinking, "Maybe now my dad will love me."

Threes, like Ones, often have a seamless quality about them; there are no rough edges. Unlike Ones, however, everything is right on the surface. As you get to know a Three, it's unlikely that you're going to plumb the depths and find more riches through time. Everything is already in view.

I was about to teach a seminar at Esalen Institute a number of years ago. As I was unloading my luggage a gentleman offered to help. While helping me unload the car, by subtle questioning he found out that I had an interest in Asian art. He then let me know that he was the biggest collector of Jain Indian art in the world; his uncle donated the Asian art wing at the Metropolitan Museum in New York; he was just at a very important auction at Christie's where he was bidding against so-and-so . . . all this in the first five minutes of introduction.

Later on in the group, talking about his business life, he said that he worked all the time, nonstop, for years at a time without a break. He said, "I would go into my company and I couldn't believe I was the only one there. I had to check to find out it was Sunday!"

Another Three, Joe Montana, was the quarterback for the San Francisco 49ers, a mythical hero who never would be forgotten in the sports circles of his community. He had taken the team to three Super Bowls. He was good-looking, had a perfect wife (also a Three), and perfect kids. His teammates referred to a magical aura that pervaded his work on the football field.

In the beginning of the 1986 season, he severely injured his back. He had a major operation, and the team officially said he might never play again and certainly not for the season. The doctor who operated on him also said he should never play football again.

In less than nine weeks, and risking permanent paralysis, he went back to playing football. When asked why — Joe Montana was a millionaire, financially set for life — he replied that he was worried about losing his job. Years later, after multiple operations on his arm, and at an age when he could gracefully retire after having a full and successful career, he instead asked to be traded to a team where he could still play for a few more years.

To the Three, life feels like a rush toward productivity. Yet, if you look beneath the hyper exterior, there is often a profound exhaustion from overwork. Threes, if they come to therapy at all — usually they are too successful and too busy — will often collapse in fatigue. A Three once said, "It's like being a car with plenty of gas and no oil."

What feels to Threes like a rush into productivity is really a rush away from feeling. Threes don't believe in the possibility of being loved. Instead they are willing to settle for validation. Rather than "Love me for who I am," the Three says, "Love me for what I've done."

Michael Jordan, one of the greatest athletes ever to play basketball, was at the peak of his career when his father was killed. Deeply affected by his father's death, he quit basketball and tried out for baseball, where he had virtually no experience and was of an age where he would be considered over the hill. When questioned about this, he explained that his father had always said that his son could be a great baseball player, that he could do anything if he really tried.

Threes have an internal state likened to that of a hamster running on a wheel in its cage. They have a sense that they must "hold the world together." There is a fear that if they stop for just a moment, the world will start to crumble.

The following Three, who is very successful in business, describes this hyperactive state:

Sometimes I would get into my office (I used to have three or four secretaries), and as soon as I would relax a little bit, I would suddenly sit up straight and think, "What am I doing resting? That's not okay." I was always doing something. Some mornings I used to get to my office, and I'd ask the people who'd report to me, "Are there any problems? No? No problems, everything's fine?" As soon as they'd get out of my office I'd start inventing problems, creating problems. Then I'd start calling people and asking for information. It was just impossible to rest. I never took vacations. I went twelve years without going on a vacation. Vacations were for silly people or lazy people. If somebody said, "Don't you think you are working too much?" I would think, "What do you mean by that?" Overload? That word just doesn't fit into my vocabulary.

If you go to a cocktail party and meet someone wearing a stethoscope, or another clear badge of his occupation, you are probably talking to a Three. Threes will tell you what they "do" within moments of beginning a conversation. They are always overachievers in one sense or another. The doctor wearing a stethoscope at the cocktail party will have his entire life reflect a certain image, and is likely to belong to the "right" country club, drive the "right" Mercedes, and have 2.3 kids.

est was a Three organization. Werner Erhard, a Sexual Three, had a spiritual insight while driving to work one day. While some people have spiritual insights and go off to meditate or to India to find a guru, Werner had an insight and produced a multimillion-dollar corporation.

est's motto was: "A World that Works for Everyone." Over and over, Werner would say, "I don't care what you're feeling; get the job done." est was great for Threes because they could reach enlightenment in two weekends and not miss any work. Of course to "prove their enlightenment" they were pressured to sell the program to the rest of the world, working in a "boiler room" filled with banks of telephones and overworked volunteers.

Passion: Deceit

The passion that runs the Three fixation is called *deceit*. This does not necessarily mean that Threes are liars, although they can be quite good at that. Rather, the deceit is in producing a role for the public. On a deep level, Threes know the role is not real, but they believe it anyway. The self-deceit of the Three lies in identification with the role as "who I really am." In a moment of rare introspection they may add, "I know, of course, it's not who I really am, but . . ." A classic example is Gwyneth Paltrow, a Sexual Three and a good actress who stopped acting because "it felt like a mask," and instead started a multi-million dollar corporation.

Threes have a psychic ability to know how they are coming across to their audience. If they pick up negative feedback, they can change what they are saying mid-sentence. I was spending some social time with a Three I know. Although his background was upper-class boarding school, Ivy League, WASP, after a short time together he started telling me Jewish jokes and dropping Yiddish punchlines! After a while I started to wonder if perhaps he was really more Jewish than me.

Threes are masters of altering themselves to meet the image that is valued by society or a particular audience. One of my students who teaches the Enneagram gave the following example of a man who was asked to sit on a panel of exemplars for point Three:

This was a highly successful businessman with a very high profile in the community. From the discussion he perceived that a "Three" who is well on his way to breaking through the fixation begins to relax and stop the high-intensity "doing." He then explained to the audience that he had quit all of his business ventures and was now staying home tending to one of his favorite hobbies. He further explained how difficult this was but that he had been succeeding. The very next day he was featured on the front page of the business section of the newspaper where it described the new business he was opening. His task of identifying with what was valued by the Enneagram audience was accomplished. He had not only deceived the audience, but unfortunately, himself as well.

At one retreat, a Three sitting on a cushion in front of the room was being "honest" with us. She let us know that for the past half hour while she spoke with us she was thinking about her socks.

She said she would never have worn those socks except that she had to wear her boots to get across campus to this room, and now she had taken her boots off. She also let us know that she knew it didn't really mean anything — she was more enlightened than that — but that she was simply reporting in a humorous way about the rising of fixation. A few minutes later, when everyone's attention was diverted, she slipped her socks off.

Childhood Setting

Threes start producing at a very early age. They usually report that they started working by the time they were five, and never stopped. Threes learn early on how to fulfill the family's (often the father's) dreams and expectations.

Threes are usually precocious as kids, looking and acting like miniature adults, often acting grown up by the time they are seven years old. Many Threes have already lost touch with their deep feelings by the time they are four or five years old. Later on in life, there is often an infantile quality when emotions are released through alcohol, drugs, or sex.

As children, Threes were rewarded for producing and always strived to produce whatever the family desired. One Three reported that as a child there were no rules. While growing up she never had a curfew or any other limits set. This was because she already instinctively knew what the rules were and followed them without any instruction.

A mother spoke of her daughter:

She was perfect even in the womb. Her birth was perfect, with no struggle. She even looked like a perfect baby. Most babies look wrinkled or hairy. People would look at her and exclaim what a perfect-looking baby she was. She never cried. At six months of age she actually spoke her name! I didn't even have to put diapers on her at night, because she never wet the bed.

Another Three reported that he always got straight A's. When his father asked him where his homework was — he would do his homework at school — he started bringing it home to do. One day he was doing his math homework as he always had, calculating the answers in his head and then writing them down. His father wanted to know where the work was, so from then on he wrote it all down.

Frequently, when I work with Threes in therapy, they do not have easy recall of childhood memories. It often takes them longer than most to begin to remember the traumas of their past. They usually report that they are constantly growing and evolving, so what happened or what they were like yesterday is irrelevant. Their interest is not in the past, but in present and future success.

Adult Threes often look young for their age. Quite often, especially in the Sexual subtype, they have a button nose and an unlined face. The face appears not to have been lived in. Howdy Doody has a classic Three face, as did John Kennedy, Shirley MacLaine, Jimmy Carter, Dick Clark, Debbie Reynolds, Doris Day, and Shirley Temple. All have (or had) faces that appear almost like masks.

Threes sell out to images of the world. What the world expects, they produce. The image they produce depends on the class and social circumstances of the family.

Threes often report a phase of acting out a rebellious stance at some point in their childhood, such as hanging out with gangs and wearing motorcycle jackets. This phase usually does not last very long. In retrospect, Threes admit that even during their rebellious phase they were just playing a role for peer-group acceptance.

It's interesting to note that most Threes report never wearing out their clothing. The desire for neatness, image, and being good, subconsciously manifests even in having shoes that never wear out.

Idealization: "I am successful."

A Three who was thrown out by his wife immediately went to his boss and told him, "I need more money because now we have two households." Using a broken marriage as a means to make more money is typical Three behavior. Everything is turned into a success. A Three discussing a bad business decision lets you know in the first sentence that he didn't think it was a good idea in the first place. He was overruled, and now will have to bail out the company.

Threes always see the glass as half full. Every circumstance is turned into a "win." They report that they always see the opportunity and benefit of every experience. Therefore, every experience is a success.

One Three was discussing his business success. When asked how successful he was, he replied that he had enough money to do whatever he wanted for the rest of his life. He then talked about a distant father who, while he was still alive, could never be found because he had a helicopter and two limousines. When asked if he competed with his father for success he said, "No, not at all. I only really became successful after he died." Was he more successful than his father? "Yes, by multiples."

Before learning this system, a Three introduced himself at a workshop by saying, "I'm very lucky and I plan to stay that way."

Talking Style: Propaganda

The talking style is called *propaganda*. Threes are always either telling you how wonderfully they are doing, or they are selling you something.

A New Age Three at a workshop managed in the first sentence of his introduction to let everyone know he was a successful publisher. He mentioned the titles of all the magazines he published, and stated that his purpose in the workshop was to become more efficient in his work. He was overheard repeating his litany of magazine titles on the lunch line a few hours later.

A Three mentioned that when unhappy as a young man, he would hide and space out by reading books. And by the way, "I donated those 30,000 books to Columbia University. And yes, I did read all of them."

I had a Three come late to a training once. None of us had ever met him before. As he walked in the door, he had to pass through the middle of a circle of about forty people sitting on the floor. As he quickly made his way to his seat, he let us know that he was a doctor and had just come from a major convention in St. Louis where he had delivered a very important paper.

Very often the talking style can sound pushy and impatient. Threes are eager to get to the bottom line. ("The bottom line" is a Three concept.) This is the home of Type A behavior. There is a sense of propaganda in everything, and an emptiness in the emotional life.

The Trap: Efficiency

The trap of *efficiency* creates polyphasic behavior. Threes are usually doing several tasks simultaneously. While driving, they will use an electric razor plugged into the cigarette lighter, listen to Berlitz German tapes, and dictate a letter over the car phone, all at the same time. Whenever you talk to Threes on the telephone, you can be sure they are doing something else as well. They usually have cordless telephone headsets so they can do the dishes, or their taxes, while on the phone.

One Three told us about taking legal pads into the bathtub. When she found she was getting them wet, she switched to a voice-activated tape recorder. Another reported eating breakfast on the toilet while shaving her legs, and dropping her food when the cell phone rang.

I once mentioned to a Three that the Day Planner must be a Three invention, and that Threes really know how to list and pri-oritize. He said, "All of that is done internally, instinctively. There is really no need to write it all down." Another Three reported that after trying to consciously slow down and do less, she found some empty space in her Day Planner and had a mild anxiety attack.

Efficiency also creates the possibility of the "ruthless climb to the top." Threes can cut people viciously and climb over them in the name of efficiency. One man, a Three who lives in Mexico, describes it this way:

I'll do whatever I have to do to get what I want to get. For example, I'm a mining engineer, and one day I decided that I had to get someplace in my career. I had to get a Masters and a Ph.D. to do it, but that was no problem. I did all that, and I started moving up. I got to the vice-presidency of a large company, Standard Oil of Mexico. I just went up and up. I would observe, "Well, now there's a guy here who has a Lear jet. What do I have to do to get a Lear jet?" Then I would just make a plan. It didn't matter if I had to work twenty-four hours a day, three hundred and sixty-five days a year, I would get there. And if somebody gets in the middle when I'm trying to get it, if I have to kill him, I kill him. [Laughs.] I never killed anybody. Nobody got in the middle. But it was possible.

The man who told the story above was questioned about whether he got the Lear jet or not, and he nonchalantly replied that it took him about a year. The converse of the ruthless climb is also a possibility; if the ship is going down, the efficient way is to leave early.

The real trap of efficiency is that when things appear to be going well, the Three is afraid to rock the boat. Rocking the boat may mean getting into deep emotions. After doing some emotional work, one Three reported, "Why muck around in that messy soup of emotions down there anyway? You want tears, I can produce tears." Threes find it much easier to pick up the appropriate emotional response from the environment than to go inside and come up with something authentic. The need for efficiency makes the discovery of real feelings hardly worth the trouble.

Defense Mechanism: Identification

While the Three may achieve the appearance of the perfect home or family, there is often a difficulty in sustaining deep, vulnerable tenderness. Since the defense is *identification*, the Three acts as if who they are is their profession, such as a doctor or a football star. They propagandize about what they do and how well they are doing it, as if that is what defines who they are.

This is the place of the workaholic. Threes identify with their jobs. Their lives are built on behaving as if they are their role. They will sometimes rewrite their histories to fit whatever they're doing at the time.

Suddenly, one day, the Three comes home from his perfect job to his perfect family, and the wife and kids are gone, and he doesn't know why. "It all seemed to be going so well," he tells his friends. There is no sense that anything is wrong because there is a lack of contact with the deeper emotions. The emotions have all been used up in production.

Avoidance: Failure

The Three's avoidance is *failure*. When Jimmy Carter (a Three) described the crash of helicopters in the Iranian desert during an aborted attempt to rescue the hostages being held in the U.S. embassy, he called it "a limited success." Failure is not in the vocabulary of the Three. If something starts to fail, he will cut it loose and move on.

In a workshop, one Three said that in childhood he was in competition with his friends and everyone in his family to see if he could be the best son, the best student, the best at sports, or whatever the arena of competition. He wanted to win at everything he did, or else he did not do it. He described this drive to achieve as follows:

If I started running, I wouldn't do it just for fun. I would start keeping my time, and then the next day it would have to be a half-minute less. I would do this until I won a race, or if there were a chance of not winning, of failure, then I would quit. I would tell myself, "I know if I do it I'll win, but I really don't feel like doing it." It's like failure is not part of my vocabulary. It's unacceptable. I can call something a learning experience, but never failure.

Threes usually keep all their options open. They are prone to setting up tentative deals. They may have twenty-five tentative deals going on all the time, so if one fails they can quickly shift the energy to another one. These people are very fast on their feet. Getting results is the bottom line.

A Three talked about his first job, which was selling class notes to the other students. He would have his friends take the notes, then type them up and make them into a package. He soon realized that his friends were not the smartest ones, so he switched friends. He became friends with the smartest students and dropped his old friends in order to succeed in his business. Consider Mark Zuckerberg, a Self-Preservation Three, and founder of Facebook, and his use of his college friends.

The Dichotomy: Overactive/Fantasy

Threes who are not overproducing are *fantasizing* about overproducing. What this means is that the Threes who are not actively engaged in life are fantasizing about their next move. If you can get a Three to stop working, as soon as he stops, he will start visualizing how he can do it even better.

Threes rarely come in for therapy because things are always going so well. But when they do come in, they are quickly, though superficially, successful clients. They are interested only in short-term therapy that produces fast results. Because of their ability to fantasize new possibilities and their desire for efficiency, they are quickly up and on their feet before getting too stuck in the deep pit of emotions.

The over-fantasizer is perfectly portrayed in a video version of the brilliant play, *Death of a Salesman*. Dustin Hoffman is perfect in the part of Willie Loman, a beaten Three who dies over-fantasizing of his imminent success, and how well-liked he is.

Subtypes

Self-Preservation: Security

The Self-preservation subtype of Three is called *security*. This means feeling secure about survival by possessing objects. Objects themselves — always brand-name, recognized objects — take on a power beyond their function.

Whoever dreamed up putting brand names on the outside of clothes was clearly a Three marketing genius. Louis Vuitton handbags represent a certain class of Three status. Conspicuous consumption is the style of Self-preservation Threes. They experience a deep security from knowing they have the best.

A Self-preservation Three was showing me around her home, which was filled with precious things. There was a breathless, almost sexual quality as she took me from room to room, admiring everything. When she took my hand, hers was sweaty from the excitement, and it was certainly not the excitement of my presence. It was our mutual gazing at her things. When I left she gave me a small shiny stone, a true token of her affection. Her Nine husband was drinking beer on the couch, oblivious to all of it.

Social: Prestige

The social subtype of Three is called *prestige*. Like the Three style, the name says it all. These people belong to the right club. Not only do they get written up in the social columns, but they also write the social columns.

In New Age circles these are the networkers and the people who teach workshops about networking. In more traditional circles, many politicians are found to be social Threes.

One social Three I know seems to know everyone in the world. He once saw my wife with a shopping bag from a fashionable boutique. He is a bachelor, with no interest whatsoever in women's clothes or fashion, except to date "the Eileen Ford models" in his younger days (as he is quick to point out). However, as soon as he noticed my wife's bag, he let us know that he was just in a limousine with the buyer for that shop and maybe he could help us get a good deal.

Publicity and the media are Social Three specialties. A Social Three I know works in the publicity department for a television station. She was once invited to have lunch with some visiting celebrities. Even though she had just come back from lunch, she eagerly accepted. She reported that she did not hear a single word that was said all through lunch because she was busy making mental lists of everyone she would call as soon as lunch was over. The idea of telling friends whom she had lunch with was much more exciting than the actual lunch.

A Social Three reported that he was the head of a large social welfare agency. He felt great pride in knowing that even as we sat there, thousands of people were being helped through the people that worked under him.

Sexual: Masculine/Feminine

When deceit leaks into the sexual arena, it is called *masculine/feminine*. This means taking on the appearance of the way society says the perfect man or perfect woman should look and act.

There is often a Playboy look of airbrushed perfection, although it may appear arid and without a lot of juice. There is sometimes a hard, shiny brittleness to it. The Beverly Hills real estate agent with perfect blonde hair, gold earrings, a gold choker, driving the perfect white Mercedes while on her car phone, is an example of this phenomenon. Annette Bening playing the realtor in *American Beauty* is a classic rendition of this fixation with Keven Spacey as the Nine husband.

Often there is a sense of androgyny as well. It is as if the Three is only acting the role. Hollywood is the home of the Sexual Three. The glamorous production of the perfect images of leading men and women have made countless Sexual Threes millionaires.

The Sexual Three fixation will manifest within the context of social class and society's expectations. A Sexual Three who grew up in a working-class neighborhood in Pittsburgh, reported that she started sewing when she was six years old. In addition to sewing and taking care of her younger brothers, she began babysitting in her spare time when she was ten.

The sewing machine became her symbol of production. From her teenage years until she married, she sewed her own clothes, as well as her family's. When she got married, she sewed all of her husband's clothes. She became the perfect model wife, within the construct of what it meant to be a perfect model wife for a working-class Pittsburgh woman. She clipped coupons, shopped carefully, and saved pennies.

Then she moved to California and acquired a new husband. He had new expectations of her. He expected her to be a professional; women were supposed to be independent. And she should be a backpacker. She became both a backpacker and a professional. She first became a bodyworker, and then a head trainer of bodyworkers. She was the first person in her family to have her own business card. She produced the image of what was required of her by her new partner.

Mick Jagger is a Sexual Three who fits the look of the '60s "sex, drugs, and rock and roll" subculture perfectly. Today he is considered a legend in the history of rock and roll music. Now in his seventies, he continues to project what is considered the right look for a rock and roll star — sexy, nonconforming hedonism. Most music stars from the '60s and '70s have grown out of their adolescent expression of rock and roll, to mellow a bit with age, and to let their musical expression mature along with their audience. Not Mick. He is still able to maintain a pace and image that is attractive to new generations of young rock fans. Here is the deceit of the Three in the sexual arena. With a seventy-something-year-old body, Jagger sings and dances like a teenager. He has produced, written, and sung a hit record album almost every year for the past five decades! Jagger's secret is to take blues and make it mainstream. Like other Sexual Threes, for example JFK and Trevor Noah, Jagger kept his baby face well into middle age.

This is not the place of great art or big breakthroughs into a dangerous new style. Sexual Threes are more pop. Their product is often a little slick, sometimes devoid of soul, but usually well done.

Consider Mick Jagger's continual successful production in the midst of a wild sex and drug life. It would have killed most of us, and did kill some early members of his band. Yet even after fifty years of this lifestyle, which finally did include giving up dangerous drugs, he is still producing albums with the Rolling Stones and touring around the world to promote them.

Additional Exemplars

Stephen Curry, the baby-faced superstar basketball player is the perfect son, perfect husband, perfect teammate, Christian and an overall good guy. He's Trevor Noah with a basketball.

Some quotes from Kanye West, a Self-Preservation Three: "I don't even listen to rap. My apartment is too nice to listen to rap in," and, "I don't know what's better gettin' laid or getting' paid."

Shirley MacLaine, also a Sexual Three, has had a successful career as a film star, starting with *Irma La Douce* when she played a sweet loving hooker in Paris. One day she had an out-of-body experience during an acupuncture session and wrote a best-selling book about it. She then had spiritual insights and went on a spiritual quest similar, in many respects, to a whole generation that has had similar insights. However, she took her spiritual insights and her trip to Peru — which many hippie spiritual seekers had done a decade before — and made them into a best-selling book and a TV special. She then did workshops to sellout crowds around the country.

Paul Newman is one of the great film stars of his generation. The man had good looks that lasted into his seventies, extreme wealth, a wonderful wife, and acclaim in his field as an actor. He also started a successful line of salad dressings and spaghetti sauce. Whatever the Three touches turns to success.

Bill Gates, a Self-Preservation Three, and Microsoft, a Self-Preservation Three corporation, represent the Three style in the '90s. The Microsoft fortune was not built on startling innovation, but rather by copying the success of Apple's interface and making it both mainstream and acceptable to the corporate culture.

Mark Zuckerberg, another Self-Preservation Three, on the other hand made his billions in a product that simulates connection and encourages sentimental feelings. He does this by objectifying relationships into commodities. In this he projects his college age psyche into a business built on imaginary emotional connection. In other words he markets emotions.

Notice the similarity in facial expressions in Bill Gates and Mark Zuckerberg. Both are baby faced proto-nerds. Very different from the revolutionary preaching and posture of Steve Jobs, a Social One.

A Social Three who thought he was a Sexual subtype asked me how to tell. I said which is the closest mirror of you, "Tom Cruise (Sexual Three)?' No. "Mick Jagger? (Sexual Three)," No. "Tom Hanks?" Yes! Ah, a Social subtype! The social subtype is fuzzier. Compare Trevor Noah to Jimmy Kimmel.

Exemplars by Subtype

Self-Preservation~Security:

Bill Gates, Mark Zuckerberg, Coco Chanel, Michael Jordan, Giorgio Armani, Arnold Palmer, Terry Cole-Whittaker, House of Gucci, Microsoft, Monaco, Hong Kong, Singapore

Social~Prestige:

Tom Hanks, Jimmy Kimmel, Johnny Carson, Sam Cook, Dan Quayle, est, Elizabeth Clare Prophet, Arsenio Hall, Bob Hope, Dick Clark, debutantes, Junior League, the "business card," Washington D.C.

Sexual~Masculine/Feminine:

Miss America, John F. Kennedy and Jackie, Denzel Washington, Tom Cruise, Matt Damon, Brad Pitt, Trevor Noah, Justin Bieber, Diana Ross, Paul Newman, Doris Day, Stephen Curry, Tiger Woods, Gavin Newsome, Emma Watson, Debbie Reynolds, Mickey Mantle, Eddie Murphy, Mary Tyler Moore, Julie Andrews, Deepak Chopra, Werner Erhard, Shirley MacLaine, Will Smith, Muhammad Ali, Ken and Barbie

Point Two: The Exteriorized Image Point

Essence:	Kindness
Holy Idea:	Freedom
Holy Path:	Humility
Chief Feature:	Flattery
Passion:	Pride
Idealization:	"I am helpful"
Talking Style:	Giving advice
Trap:	Will
Defense Mechanism:	Repression
Avoidance:	Needs
Dichotomy:	Militant/Libertine
Subtypes:	Self-Preservation~Me First Social~Ambition Sexual~Aggression/Seduction

Point Two is the exteriorized version of point Three. All the image points suffer from a lack of self-worth, coming from a belief that they cannot be loved for themselves. The Three develops the strategy of trying to be loved for what is produced. Twos, on the other hand, want to be loved for their helpfulness and specialness. They are the helpers, the codependents, the overworking mothers, and the self-sacrificing wives as Self-preservations. The socials are the stars like Dolly Parton and Little Richard.

In general, rather than working on the environment to fulfill their needs for survival, Twos work on another person, who then works on the environment. Thus, Twos are generally the most dependent of the personality types.

When they dress up, Twos can often look like little girls in mommy's clothing. They might have giant eyelashes, big bows, puffy sleeves, spike-heeled sandals with glitter, or, like the maid in the film, *La Cage Aux Folles*, a little maid's apron and a bare bottom. Dolly Parton and Tammy Faye Bakker are examples of glittery, big-eyelash Twos, and Liberace is a male version. Whereas the Sexual Two's are the seducers, with Elvis being a male sequined version.

From the outside, this strategy appears to be rather successful. The Two is the idealized woman in Western society, the perfect supermom, wife, secretary, friend and lover who is always willing to deny her own needs in order to take care of someone else.

Twos seem to be loved and admired, and to get all the love they need in return for their selfless service. And that is the rub. The service is never really selfless. It is generated out of a feeling of deep self-hatred. The Two is desperately trying to gain love and self-esteem by taking care of someone else. They rarely have the energy to take care of themselves. They may fix a gourmet candle-light meal for their fiance, or a family feast with a dozen courses, but when left alone with no one to take care of but themselves, they may find themselves eating out of cans or forgetting to eat altogether.

For the Two, giving help is an extraction process. It is an attempt to milk self-worth back from the world in exchange for services (supposedly) freely given. The Two is perhaps the most cloaked form of prostitution on the Enneagram. It is also the one most overlooked because many of us enjoy being taken care of by Twos.

One major pattern of the Two personality is flattery. When I explained this once to a Two, she blurted out, "But it's always important to make the boy feel better." That is the essence of the Two's fixation. In making you feel better, they get their self-worth.

Underneath the goodness, sweetness, and light, however, is a stainless steel interior. In truth, you can never make up to the Twos everything they have done for you. No one can take care of Twos as well as they have taken care of someone else. And just below the surface, they are painfully aware of this fact.

Twos are the most dependent of the personality fixations. Even in the social subtype, where we have the manifestation of the "star," there is a sense that the star's manager is a key ingredient of the show. The world knew Elvis Presley's manager Colonel Tom Parker. His power is that of the stable foundation from which the performers move. The tragedy of Two stars like Elizabeth Taylor is the lack of this stable "Daddy." In contrast, this is seldom the case for Three stars, who are quite capable of taking care of themselves.

A male Two described it in this way:

It is like I am living underwater in a sea of emotions. I am floating through it, and looking out through my goggles, and I see you all floating out there. I then do my best to attract you so that you will see me and appreciate me.

Passion: Pride

The passion that runs the Two is *pride*. When most other points hear and recognize their fixation, they immediately understand the passion that is running them. This has never been my experience with Twos, who are often more in touch with their anger and resentment. They know they have feelings of being used or of not receiving love. They are also clearly in touch with their love of being helpful. Yet, if pride is mentioned, there is usually a blank look of confusion. "But I enjoy taking care of other people," the Two will respond. There is almost never a deeper awareness of the pride that runs the machine.

A clear example of the pride that underlies the Two's behavior was described by this workshop leader:

Each morning of my month-long training I lead a sitting meditation. I always get to the meditation room at least fifteen minutes early to make sure everything is in order, and I am already meditating when the group arrives. I do this because it feels like my responsibility to the group and because it feels good.

One morning my clock stopped, and I arrived an hour late. I opened the door thinking I was early, and the room was already filled with people meditating. The first feeling that arose and overwhelmed me was shame. As I examined it, I realized I wasn't upset over missing my own meditation, which I love and need. Rather, I was feeling humiliated. I realized that pride had been running my game all along.

As one woman reported, "I know that I can win you over very easily. I can do things for you before you even know that you need them done. Washing, ironing, cooking, no problem. But I am waiting for you to say that I am the best—the best mother, the best lover, the best wife."

A male Two reported, "When you are the boss and you are the best and everyone is always kowtowing to you, you start to feel like they are right. You don't take the time to see what is running deeper."

The other side of pride is resentment. There is a joke about the mother who bought her son two ties for Christmas. The next time she saw him, he was wearing one of the ties. She said, "What's the matter? You don't like the other one?"

Childhood Setting

Traditionally, the Two was Daddy's little girl. These were the little girls with the curls who were cute, funny, and curled in your lap with a coquettish smile. I also know many male Twos, who also learned very early how to be sweet and wrap Mommy around their little fingers. For gay male Twos, the issue is being Daddy's little boy.

A male Two reported that by age five he was taking care of his younger brother and sister. He would sit and rock the cradle and keep them both quiet. He diapered his baby sister and started cooking for the family by the time he was seven. He is a baker by trade now and says, "I love it! I love taking care of people."

Another Two reported having the very clear memory of lying in her crib, needing attention. Yet, she would never cry because her mother was already so busy with the other five children; she didn't want to be a burden.

This same Two said she started dancing at four years old and won her first medal at five. She kept dancing and winning medals until she was eleven. She said she was willing to do whatever it took to keep the spotlight on her. She started cooking when she was three, and has scars on her hand from an accident she had at five while making custard for her family. She started washing dishes as soon as she could stand up; she would stand on a chair to wash them. When I asked how old she was when she started sewing, she said she didn't start using the sewing machine until she was five. Before that it was just hand sewing.

Another female Two recalled:

I learned to be funny and cute to get Daddy's attention so he would have fun with me. That was the only thing that really worked. I'm sure it caused difficulty because my mother was so removed and so empty and quiet, she must have been jealous.

This observation is profound for a Two. She won Daddy's love in competition with Mother. And Mother, never being able to voice her loss publicly and sometimes not consciously aware of it, became resentful of her child.

Quite often Twos come into therapy with a feeling of deep connection with their fathers and an unhappy relationship with their mothers. When questioned, they really don't know the root of the conflict with their mothers. When they explore it, they often find that winning Daddy's love was the unconscious issue.

Another female Two said:

I was very aware that my father was enamored of me, and he was. He was also very enamored of my mother. She was a full person. I was just totally innocent and unaware of any kind of sexual stuff until somebody turned me on to sex. It wasn't until I was about eighteen or nineteen that I had the first conscious thought of any kind of sexual attraction between my father and me.

Then it wasn't until my twenties that I was aware of any possible conflict in our family. I always had the sense of having an idyllic childhood. Ours was the family everybody wished they had. The resentments, jealousies, and competition in our family were very subtle, because everything was so "good." People were really lively, happy, and affectionate. Things were very couched. My mother's sadness and resentment were couched in sweetness.

Being naive about sexuality is an appropriate description; this is actually a pre-genital fixation. It is not a sexual attraction to Daddy at all. Sex isn't really the issue. For Twos, wanting to be held and cuddled is usually more important than sex; sex is often a way to keep their partner or to give them what they seem to want.

A counterexample to the above was shared by a Sexual Two. She said her parents had her dancing and entertaining sailors by the time she was four or five years old. At that point she felt her sexuality and loved it. She has been sexually active ever since, with a huge variety of partners.

Our close cousins the Bonobos are a matriarchal society based on sex. Sex is used for food, security and relationships. It is a give in order to get society where everyone enjoys the perks, as even the lowest members have their pleasures fulfilled.

Idealization: "I am helpful."

The idealization of the Two is *"I am helpful,"* and indeed they are. Unlike Eights, who will tell you what is wrong with you ("You look ridiculous in those clothes!"), or Ones, who might preach ("You know, respectable women of your age shouldn't be walking around town looking like that"), Twos will say, "You are looking really healthy today. And by the way, I know a place that sells clothes for half-off. They have the most darling dress there, and I know that you would look fabulous in it. It would definitely show the real you."

A Two came in to housesit once for a couple going to Europe on a three-month tour. Because they had a home office, and the person who was supposed to be responsible for running the office left, the Two "helped out." Within days of the couple's leaving, the Two learned how to run the computer, take orders on the phone, ship out products, and pay all the bills.

When the book they were selling ran out while the couple was still in Europe, the Two took it upon herself to contact the publisher and arrange for a new printing of the book. All of this with no background experience, training, or pay. She was just being helpful.

One woman reported, "I did everything. We were married for eight years and I did everything. I did the books, the advertising, running the business as well as everything at home. I got up at 5:30 every morning to make his breakfast. The man did not do cereal."

Talking Style: Giving Advice

The talking style that fits so neatly with this idealization is *giving advice*. Twos may find themselves in the position of Dear Abby, the very famous newspaper columnist to whom people wrote with personal problems.

People are forever telling Twos about their problems, and the Two intimately joins in with helpful advice. They are the masters of establishing rapport with others and entering into another's reality. Once in rapport, the Two skillfully steers by giving advice.

This can, however, have disastrous consequences, since the Two can be in rapport with everyone. One couple who was having marital difficulties had a Two friend. The couple was temporarily separated, living in different states, and both were in touch with the Two. She advised both of them as best friends. However, when they got together and compared notes they were shocked. "She said that to you! But she told me the opposite."

The classic example of Two advice-giving is Dolly Parton in the movie, *Straight Talk*, when she plays the role of a woman who makes a career of being sweet and helpful, and giving good advice, while falling for Sexual Eight men.

The Trap: Will

The trap is called *will*. This trap feeds into the Two's blindness about the pride which actually runs the machine. Since their own needs are repressed, Twos have the illusion that they have a free will to do something for you. The trap of will is the creation of the illusion of choice.

To truly have will in any situation, one must have choice. Since self-worth and love are on the line whenever a Two is helpful, there can be no true will involved. The illusion of will becomes the trap of repressing one's own needs in order to take care of another.

This trap becomes apparent when Twos break into their inevitable rage. They will rant and rave about all they have done and how used up they feel, with a list that may go back for years. This reveals the falsehood that they were helpful out of free will and free choice.

Defense Mechanism: Repression

The defense mechanism is called *repression*. Twos have repressed their own needs to such an extent that they are no longer aware of them. They are aware only of the desire to take care of others.

I was once walking uphill with a Two, at a rather brisk pace. We were in perfect sync, as we walked up the hill, stride for stride. After about fifteen minutes, I suddenly realized that I was in much better shape, and asked her, "Is this pace too fast for you?" Her immediate breathless reply was, "How is it for you?"

One Two, after complaining about doing everything, both running the business and the home, and then saying she was terrified to enter into that sort of relationship again, finished by saying, "I love taking care of people. I really do. It is what I really love."

Avoidance: Needs

The avoidance is called *needs*: Twos avoid their own needs. The avoidance of needs, the trap of will, and the defense mechanism of repression all work together as a very tight unit to keep the Two squeezed into the nurturing machine. It is as if someone consciously programmed the perfect slave, who avoids his own needs, represses his own desires, and believes that taking care of the master is a choice made of his own free will.

From the outside, the Two does not look like a slave at all. As a matter of fact, other people (women in particular) are often jealous that they are not of this fixation. They are jealous that, try as they may, they can never be such a selfless helper or such a perfect, kind, and pretty, loving person. The truth is that Twos have avoided their own needs in order to serve. Because of this, Twos can truly empathize with other people. They can reproduce the emotional state of the person they're talking with, as they go into sympathy with them.

The Dichotomy: Militant/Libertine

The dichotomy in Two is called *militant/libertine*. Very different styles of relating to the world will be produced, depending on which side of the dichotomy a Two is manifesting. Nancy Reagan was a militant Two who ran a tight ship. She steered her husband, Ronald Reagan, around like a prop. She is very different from Dolly Parton or Elizabeth Taylor, who are examples of libertine

Twos. The difference in body types between Nancy Reagan and Dolly Parton seems to hold for this dichotomy in general. Militant Twos are often tightly wrapped, thin, with the appearance of leaning toward the One fixation. The libertines, on the other hand, are often voluptuous in body and style.

While the militant Two is often the efficient executive secretary, the libertine Two may be a prostitute or biker's girl. In almost all cases they are considered pretty with a young, sweet face. The militant Two is often the real power behind the relationship, while the libertine Two may find herself in an abusive relationship.

Culture

Thailand and Bali are both Two cultures. Thailand is called the land of smiles. The men and women are beautiful, helpful and friendly. It is impossible to directly say "no" in Thai culture. There are dozens of ways of saying "yes" but meaning "no" so as to remain friendly and helpful. And Thailand is famous for its massage industry, sex scene, and marital affairs being a common way of relating. The little mirrors and curlicues that adorn the royal palace and the temples, the style of Thai architecture is a Two style, of buildings wearing big eyelashes and glittery frills.

Bali on the other hand is a social Two culture. Babies are held and not put on the ground for the first 105 days after their birth, as they are considered too sacred to touch the earth. Once they do hit the ground, a baby can wander anywhere and be taken care of by other villagers. Noted for their friendliness and massage, the Balinese also gave us the term "running amok," which is the Two response to stress.

Subtypes

Self-Preservation: Me First

The Self-preservation subtype of the Two is called *"Me first."* At first glance, this may seem like an odd name for a group of people who are always the power behind the throne (such as the executive secretary or the wife of the boss). Self-preservation Twos never want to be identified as the boss. They are much more comfortable as the boss's advisor. They run the show from behind the scenes.

These people can be extremely hard-working, obsessively working seven days a week, twelve hours a day, as loyal assistants. A Self-preservation Two boasted that her boss once signed a company check and the bank returned it because they only recognized her version of his signature.

Because they have given away so much of themselves, these people assume pride of place. They feel justified in cutting in line at buffets or movies. If there is not enough food to go around, Self-preservation Twos will get theirs. And do not try to eat from their plates! Many Self-preservation Twos have said they might cut your finger off. After having given so much, they feel entitled to such selfishness. As one man is fond of saying about his many relationships with Twos, "They love to give, but when they want something, you'd better make those credit cards smoke!"

Social: Ambition

If the Self-preservation Two is the power behind the throne, the ambition Two is on the throne. This is the place of the star.

They are not necessarily stars in the Hollywood sense (though some of them are, such as Elizabeth Taylor and Dolly Parton). One Two I know is a physical therapist. Her favorite time is when the head of the clinic is out of the office and she can shine. I was in the clinic after a knee operation. She directed her team of helpers to massage me, icing my knee and making sure I had plenty of towels and was comfortable. She is the star of taking care of her patients.

I once flew in the upper cabin of a 747 jumbo jet in the early days. The male steward was a Social Two. He had sixteen people to care for on a flight from San Francisco to Japan. He had a little staging area where he stood watching over us. He knew what everyone wanted to drink after the first round and made sure our glasses were always full. After a short time, my companion and I didn't want any more Perrier, yet we felt obligated to drink so we wouldn't hurt his feelings.

Another Social Two was an artist's model. She loved to pose naked and then go around to look at the various pictures. She loved the evidence of the attention paid to her.

Liberace, the pianist in sequins, is the classic male Social Two, as are Little Richard and John Travolta, dancing to the song "Staying Alive."

Sexual: Aggression/Seduction

If the Self-preservation Two is the power behind the throne, and the social Two is on the throne, the Sexual Two seduces the throne. *Aggression/ seduction* is the act of seducing power. Sexual Twos experience love as the melting of resistance. Once the resistance is melted, the relationship quickly gets boring.

A Sexual Two I know has had four husbands, and children by five different fathers. The number of lovers she has had is beyond counting.

These are the most seductive people on the Enneagram. Twos — Sexual Twos in particular — are often accused of being teases and of leading men on. But they are always surprised by this accusation. There is often no conscious awareness of what effect they produce. When they first meet you, and frequently thereafter, the sexual Two will touch you. It may be just a light touch on the arm, but undoubtedly a physical connection will be made.

Sexual Twos will walk into a room and immediately sense where the power is. They will then move towards the power and seduce it. A lot of groupies are Sexual Twos. A Sexual Two I know keeps a count of the gurus she has known.

Leaving Las Vegas is the story of a Sexual Two, played by Elisabeth Shue of the same fixation. She portrays a prostitute who finds another man as soon as her pimp leaves her. The man she settles with is an alcoholic Nine played by Social Nine Nicholas Cage. The biggest scene of the movie is when she pours whiskey over her naked breasts and pushes his head into her. We know that this is his fantasy, not hers, but she is willing to degrade herself to please him.

I was teaching an Enneagram workshop at my home a number of years ago. During the break, a beautiful, young woman in a clinging jersey got me in a corner, placed her hand on my chest, looked meltingly into my eyes and asked, "Could you help me discover what fixation I am?" My wife came over and told her.

Additional Exemplars

Nancy Reagan was a good example of the Self-preservation militant Two. Various memoirs of close White House aides have confirmed what we already knew; she ran the presidential show. It was Nancy who had the first national security advisor fired. It was at Nancy's insistence that the White House chief of staff had to go. Her husband Ronnie was a Nine and started on the left with his first wife and married a right-wing wife and became right wing.

Many American presidents were helped and guided into power by their Two wives. Rosalyn Carter added a depth of caring for humanity to Jimmy Carter's presidency, as Lady Bird supported Lyndon Baines Johnson. This is very different from Hillary Clinton, who is a puritan Eight, and an aggressive leader of the team.

Elvis Presley, a male Two, idolized his mother and always took care of her first. He gave away Cadillacs to his friends, and in taking care of his teenage wife, refrained from sex in the beginning of their relationship.

Exemplars by Subtype

Self-Preservation~Me First:

Nancy Reagan, Lady Bird Johnson, Rosanna Arquette, Rosemary Woods, Rosalyn Carter, Rosa Parks, Our Gal Friday, Bali

Social~Ambition:

Dolly Parton, Elizabeth Taylor, Little Richard, Magic Johnson, George Stephanopoulos, Tammy Faye Bakker, Mia Farrow, Liberace, John Travolta, Bert Parks, Betty Boop, Carol Channing

Sexual~Aggression/Seduction:

Elvis Presley, Drake, Geena Davis, Elisabeth Shue, Sissy Spacek, Smokey Robinson, Fawn Hall, Liv Ullman, Sam Cooke, Jessica Rabbit, Thailand

Point Four: The Interiorized Image Point

Essence:	Joy
Holy Idea:	Origin
Holy Path:	Equanimity
Chief Feature:	Melancholy
Passion:	Envy
Idealization:	"I am elite"
Talking Style:	Lamentation
Trap:	Authenticity
Defense Mechanism:	Introjection
Avoidance:	Feeling lost
Dichotomy:	Analytic/Disoriented
Subtypes:	Self-Preservation~Dauntless Social~Shame Sexual~Competition

The interiorized version of point Three is point Four. This is the imploded version of the hysteric personality. While the Two has pride of place, the Four feels the shame of being out of place. Four never really feels at home, never really feels in relaxed harmony with the environment. Twos have the pride of position, while Fours feel imploded. Fours often seem to be waiting for life to begin.

Fours, like Fives, are at a point at the bottom of the Enneagram where they are aware of a black hole inside. They experience this hole as a wound and a loss, as if something is missing. This black hole is their proof that they are tragically marked, and that they are special. Fours will often drive away the person they love before he gets too close and uncovers the tragedy of this dark wound. A good example of this behavior is *The French Lieutenant's Woman*, who spends years alone on the cliffs, longing for her lover, and then runs away when he comes near. Scarlett O'Hara in *Gone with the Wind* is another example of the Four character loving the man more the farther away he is.

Fours by nature are dancers, artists, and workshop junkies. They are often people who continually work to improve themselves. The Four fixation is the home of cosmetic surgery and the "perm." Fours love to dress with unique style. They can spend hours on makeup that "looks natural" and will complement an expensive, natural fiber, layered look. Fours may dress out of free boxes and wear secondhand clothes, but their dress will always make an understatement of style. Or they may shop at the best shops in the world and spend hours attempting to look as if the outfit were casually thrown together without thought.

Where the Two won Daddy's love, the Four feels the loss of the father. Both female and male Fours experience Daddy's loss, or the loss of the strong parent, and internalize the experience to mean there is something wrong with them. Fours then create themselves to be the person Daddy would love. The feeling of the loss and the defense of introjection create the natural "drama queens" of the world.

Feeling themselves to be "marked" by the loss, and therefore unique, Fours may develop a sense of elitism and the attitude that "normal rules don't apply to me." Fours revel in their melancholy. Kathleen Speeth described this as "an exquisite cut flower in a fine crystal vase, beautiful but already dying and cut off at the root... yearning to return to the garden."

Fours are love addicts. There is a sense of never being able to be filled up. You must prove your love to them every day, several times a day. And you must prove it in different ways, always coming up with something new. Fours will constantly test you with, "What have you done for me lately?" There is a feeling of having already suffered so much, no one can ever make it up to them. One Four said, "It isn't that you aren't making it up to me, it isn't 'makeup-able,' because I've never gotten over the original abandonment."

"You never really loved me!" may be lamented or shouted out of the clear blue, and another round on the emotional roller coaster has begun. Fours have a sense of living emotionally, full tilt. They tend to be attracted to Eights because they both have explosive emotional intensity.

Traditional Japan is a Four culture. At the heart of Japanese culture, there is a deep sense of being cut off from the mainland root of China. This sense of deep inferiority in relationship to the Chinese pervades the Japanese aesthetic. The Japanese took the best of Chinese culture and made it better. The kimono, the tea ceremony, Zen, Go, acupuncture, architecture, and gardening all have their roots in China, but were perfected by the Japanese.

The favorite season in Japan is autumn; it is the exquisite dying that the Four cherishes. The favorite emotion in Japanese culture is unrequited love. Even the national song to the cherry blossom is sung as a lament as the beautiful cherry blossom falls to its death. The Japanese national myth is of the Eight samurai and the Four geisha and the tragedy of unrequited love.

The Japanese garden is an attempt to take nature and make it "more natural." The best Japanese garden looks completely natural, as if man had never been there. Careful manipulation and conscious placement of each rock, as well as daily grooming of each leaf, achieve this effect. In this same way, Fours painstakingly create each fold of their personality and dress, to achieve a sense of casual naturalness.

But since the cultural models are the samurai and the geisha, emotions are shameful and many couples have never said, "I love you," out of a deep sense of shame.

Passion: Envy

Driven by the passion of *envy*, the Four feels a deep lack of self-worth and need for constant comparison with others. There is a sense that "mine isn't as good." They feel so damaged that for them the grass is always greener on the other side of the fence. Someone else always has it better, seems to be happier, or seems to have the perfect relationship. Just as Freudian psychology can be seen as deriving from a Six man (Freud) working with "hysteric women," the concept of penis envy must have been similarly developed by a Four. Here, a female Four at a workshop shares the following:

I feel the envy with my sister. She is always very successful. She does everything perfectly, and I am always striving to be as good as her, to make as much money, to be as successful, to have the right career.

When I see couples together, they always look like they are more loving together, are doing better, than the relationship I am in. It's like I am all the time wanting something that isn't quite within reach.

From another Four:

Envy for me is that people have something I haven't got — thinner legs, taller, fuller lips, their hair is nicer, you name it. I'll look and say, "Gee, I wish I had lips like that."

There is also a sense that there isn't enough. A Four may love looking through someone else's home, noticing how they compare. They may have a compulsion to over-consume, to buy more and more material possessions, particularly clothes. This is the home of the shopper, and often the home of the shoplifter, becoming involved in petty crimes such as stealing make-up. *Madame Bovary* is one of the best examples of this fixation, as she shopped her husband into the poorhouse.

The farther away something is, the better it looks, and the closer it gets, the worse it looks. The Four's life is often a series of crushes on people or things they strive to possess. Once they possess something, however, it turns to ashes in their hands. As

Groucho Marx once said, "I would never belong to a club that would have me as a member."

When caught in repose, Fours often seem to have a deep sadness in their eyes, like *The French Lieutenant's Woman*, out alone on the cliffs, longing and waiting. Life was better in the past, or will be better in the future. There is melancholy for the way it used to be, or longing for the knight in shining armor who has never come. But the closer the knight gets, the more a Four sees his warts and imperfections.

Fours experience a feeling of great longing. They believe they have deeper feelings than the rest of us. What is true is that they are probably able to act out the widest range of felt emotions. While they do have deep feelings, they also tend to exaggerate. This is the place of melodrama and histrionics: "Nobody suffers like I do."

If you go shopping with a Four and buy a sweater, she will immediately feel the need to buy one too. If you're in a relationship with a Four and you have a lover, the Four will undoubtedly need to have two lovers. A Four described it as "never having enough and always needing to get more. Jealousy for me is a feeling of taking it all personally. It all has to do with me."

Childhood Setting

The childhood of the Four is the story of the lost garden. While Self-preservation Fours often feel the loss of connection and begin their suffering in the womb, most Fours report a period of infant or childhood bliss. As children they basked in the garden of love, feeling cared for and loved. They saw Daddy as the sun that shone and nourished them. But at some point they were expelled.

The classic story is of a little girl who's crazy about her daddy, and he's crazy about her. They play, they hug, and they are very affectionate. Then, at some point, the father becomes aware of his feelings of sexuality toward his daughter and becomes frightened.

One day she hops in his lap and he says, "No, get down." As far as she is concerned, something is wrong, and it is her fault that she has been expelled.

The Four feels fatally scarred by this pulling away, this loss of love. It means, "There is something wrong with me." In both male and female Fours, the fixation seems to revolve around loss of love from the father. Some Self-preservation Fours have described womb experiences in which they knew they were not wanted by either parent. They already felt unloved and took it personally. A female Four describes her experience of feeling this loss of love from her father, and taking it personally throughout her life:

Ever since I can remember I have felt that there was something wrong with me. When I was young, I felt that I was Daddy's little girl until maybe age four or five. Around this time, he started drinking. Since then, there has been a sense of emotional abandonment throughout my life.

It really shows up in relationships with men. When I am living alone, I feel stronger, more centered, more together. But as soon as I get into relationship with a man, I go right to sleep, the veil comes down, and suddenly I feel worthless and unlovable and needy.

While frequently there is also a lack of maternal nurturing, Fours most often fixate on the loss of the father. The exception to this is when the mother is perceived as the dominant partner. In order to regain the garden, Fours have to be so unique that the rules don't apply. As soon as they reach late puberty, they usually act out the worst behavior and relationships their parents could imagine. They often start sexual relationships extremely early, and will date interracially if that is the family phobia.

If the Four's parent is a crusader against drugs, there is a good chance the Four will experiment with drugs and flaunt it. It is not rebellion, however. This point never crosses to the nonconformist side of the Enneagram, even though initially Fours may appear to be the most nonconformist of people. They will dress outrageously, do and say outrageous things, but it is all within the context of being part of the family. They are actually addicted to their parents and for a long time they will try to prove, "I am so special that I deserve admittance back to the garden."

The sense of loss of the garden creates a longing. The loss gets re-created over and over again as Fours fall in love, create emotional blowups, and leave. Then they long for the next relationship or regret what they have ruined. Either way, relationships are longed for and then destroyed, endlessly. Fours often feel they have to blow up the relationship before it gets too deep and the lover discovers the scar, the tragic flaw, and leaves. In childhood they fear and create issues of abandonment, issues that persist throughout their lives.

Idealization: "I am elite."

The conceit of Fours is that they are not only unique — which is true for everyone — but they are also special. The idealization is, *"I am elite.* After they made me, they broke the mold." There's an elitism and a separateness. But on the other side of that, there is also a feeling of being "not as good as," which fuels their envy.

Fours are often artists and travel in elite circles of intellectuals, Bohemians, or other unique fringe groups. One woman described moving to Greenwich Village so that she could wear black turtlenecks, smoke cigarettes, and read Beaudelaire in the cafes.

Talking Style: Lamentation

The talking style of the Four is called *lamentation.* I sometimes have people close their eyes, ignore the words, and just listen to the emotional tone being transmitted. The weepy sadness of the Four comes through at every unguarded moment.

This is the place of gossip and relating tales of woe. Fours can spend hours on the telephone with their friends, lamenting their relationships and how life is treating them.

Since this is an image point, the Four may also respond quickly to the mood of the person they are with. They may be funny, bright, and often unconsciously witty. This is especially true when they are talking about something other than the tragedy of their own lives.

Judy Garland was a Four whose lamentation saturates all of her public performances. Billie Holiday is another example of a Four whose music reflected the sad tragedy of her life. *Madame Bovary* is one of the best examples of this fixation, both in print and on film.

The Trap: Authenticity

The trap is called *authenticity*. The Four point of view is that style is everything. A Four would never do anything to betray mood, manners, or style. I have heard stories from Fours of sitting for hours, while having to urinate badly, but not wanting to interrupt the ongoing dialogue. A Four I know would never use the toilet at her lover's apartment because the very thought was too gross. I have watched Fours completely make up details and events in their stories because it fits the mood, not the facts.

Fours take hours to put on makeup so that it looks as if they are not wearing any makeup at all. At Esalen, lots of women don't wear makeup, but the Fours almost always do. It is so well done, however, that their faces appear to be natural. They take a long time, paying conscious attention to minor details, in order to achieve this understated artistic feat. It is an attempt to be an authentic, natural, little girl/woman. This style is quite different from that of women who wear very high heels and obvious makeup.

Fours consider themselves unique, original, and natural. They don't want you to know they had an eye job, or that they're wearing makeup, or that their hair is permed. "It is just a natural expression of who I am." Fours hate phoniness; the worst thing they can say about you is that you are a phony.

One thing to notice in Fours is their unique dressing style, often in their shoes. Female Fours usually have great boots. Male Fours also quite often have a sense of expressing their uniqueness in footwear. I know a male Four who leads workshops. I had the first hint of his fixation from his sandals, which were the most unique shoes I had ever seen. There was nothing loud, glaring, or calling for attention; rather, there was a uniqueness of style and quiet attention to detail. His shirts were also different from the t-shirts everyone else was wearing, with a special cut to the sleeve. He later said he was never good enough for Daddy. He had been an athlete — even captain of the football team — but it never really got his dad back for him. He felt he was never good enough.

Another Sexual Four in one of my workshops was by far the best-dressed person in the room each day. He dressed not in a way that would call attention to himself, although he did have his own powder-blue meditation cushion. He chose unique patterns in his socks and displayed a sense of color and style. Even when he wore mismatched socks (as a casual, hip substyle), each sock was both unique and in perfect harmony with its unmatched mate.

Defense Mechanism: Introjection

The defense mechanism of the Four is *introjection*, the taking on of others' emotions as their own. Feeling unlovable, scarred, and un-worthy, they take all the negative emotions from the environment and swallow them whole. Where Eights deny everything and Sixes project out into the environment, Fours take on all negativity as their own. This can lead to psychosomatic disorders, as well as emotional traumas and depression. This is a rather ironic defense mechanism: rather than defending against the negativity in the world, Fours believe that everything is their fault. The following story was shared by a Four:

I know I take in a lot of feelings from others. I didn't realize this until later in my life. At the age of twenty-one, I had my gallbladder removed. I later found out that gallbladder disease typically happens to somebody who is swallowing feelings. I was a classic example of this kid who took on all the feelings of the family. I grew up in a pretty intense household. By the time I was twenty-one years old, I had a disease that normally a sixty-or seventy-year-old person gets. It was pretty extreme.

Living from their emotional body, Fours are very sensitive to the emotional environment in which they live. A Four will walk into a group of people and immediately become aware of the emotional atmosphere. This introjection of negative emotions may lead to health difficulties and emotional imbalance.

Avoidance: Feeling Lost

The avoidance of the Four is called *feeling lost.* Fours have two conditions in their makeup that tend to feed this avoidance. First, they feel uprooted and therefore basically disoriented. Second, and more importantly, they have a deep sense that there is a black hole of emptiness. Four is the place of eating disorders; bulimics often talk about using food to try to fill the black hole.

Fours are frequently pseudo-oriented in time and space; their orientation is almost always in relationship to someone else. Being in a relationship is a strategy for avoiding the feeling of being lost. They attempt to fill the black hole with love relationships.

The Dichotomy: Analytic/Disoriented

The dichotomy in Four is called *Analytic/Disoriented.* As with all the fixations, both poles of the dichotomy are always present, but one side of the dichotomy is presented as the ego mask for facing the world.

The disoriented Four represents the classic stereotype of the "dizzy woman." Whether it is a physical disorientation and a real problem following directions or maps, or an inability to follow the flow of a conversation, the disorientation seems to have two roots. The first root is in their feeling of being cut off. The other is that they are often so involved in their own emotional drama, there is not much attention left for the rest of the world.

Unlike the disoriented Four, the analytic Four can seem exceedingly mental at times. In an effort to avoid the sense of feeling lost, the analytic Four attempts to stay in the realm of thought. Sometimes male Fours, because they wish to avoid the deep feelings that are not considered "manly," appear on the surface to be analytical. However, just below the surface is the full torrent of the Four's emotional sea. It often bubbles up at inappropriate times, creating ripples in their "cold analytic" posture. In the words of a male Four:

I have this feeling that I don't fit. It is a feeling of being out of place, that something is missing. It seems tragic. As a child, the feeling was there all the time. It didn't matter what I was doing. Whether I was popular or unpopular, quiet or outgoing, it was always like I was on the wrong planet, in the wrong place, wrong movie, wrong book. Like I didn't belong here.

Subtypes:

Self-Preservation: Dauntless

The *dauntless* Four is a person determined to succeed in spite of his tragic flaw. These are people who fiercely and furiously attempt to drive their way to success. Bette Davis, Orson Welles, and Peter Lorre all are dauntless Fours, with a "bug-eyed" look of pressure behind their eyes. Though not all dauntless Fours have this look, it represents the style. Dauntless means "I will prevail."

There can also be a style of living dangerously on the edge. Fours, like Eights, feel that normal societal rules don't apply. Energy enlivens Fours when they are on the edge, and there is an issue of survival. They are often very high-energy, creative people.

And yet Fours can have the quality of a drunk on a tightrope. Francis Ford Coppola is an example of this phenomenon. Even though he had major financial success with his *Godfather* films, and millions of dollars in the bank, he was willing to risk it all on the next roll.

In their first impression, Dauntless Fours can appear to be Threes. They can appear to have a hard-edged, slightly brittle drive for success. But the drive is not coming from the Three's sense of efficiency; it is coming from the sense of being flawed. If you touch them a little bit deeper, sadness usually wells up. There is a sense of not really being good enough, of being tragically flawed.

Steve Martin, dancing, spinning, and joking his way into your heart, is a good example of a Self-preservation Four who almost looks like a Three. His best early comedy was based on being the "lonely guy." In his classic first film, *The Jerk*, he plays a white boy growing up in a poor Southern black family, not aware that he is adopted, but knowing that he is somehow "different." Another such role is Cyrano de Bergerac. His best roles are the lovable sad-eyed clowns.

Social: Shame

Social Fours often exhibit a disoriented style of being in the world. They seem to move through life in a miasmic cloud of confusion. This is the most imploded point on the Enneagram, due to a deep sense of lack of place. The *shame* that the Social Four feels pervades all areas of life.

The gay scene in the '80s in the San Francisco area had the style of the social Four. Perhaps this explains why Judy Garland is one of the gay community's icons. It is a culture of great food, great style in clothes, and a tragic romanticism.

It is rare to find a Social Four who makes it onto the public stage; Judy Garland was a rare example. Kate Wolf is another example of a Social Four who sang songs of lamentation and died a tragic, early death. Johnny Depp has this fixation as well. In one of his early films, *What's Eating Gilbert Grape*, he does a remarkable takeoff on Buster Keaton, another Social Four.

I had a client who was a Social Four and fancied himself an opera singer. When I met him, he was in his forties; with his facelift starting to go, he was already on the edge of being too old to start a new career. As each audition came up, he developed a cold, or his vocal chords were sore. He made his living giving voice lessons, but was always preparing for the day when his career would begin.

One Social Four I know makes a good living as a psychotherapist. However, she squeaks by wearing old clothes and eating frugally, while saving all her earnings, which she will spend when her life "begins."

Sexual: Competition

Competition in Sexual Fours may have its roots in penis envy. They have a sense of competition in all relationships, but particularly with their mate. Sexual Fours are always sizing up their competition and one-upping their mates. If their partner buys something, Sexual Fours have a burning need to rush out and buy something themselves.

These are the best dressers on the Enneagram. An enormous amount of time is spent on personal grooming and shopping to create a casual, natural look. Where Social Fours may live in secondhand clothes, waiting for their lives to begin, Sexual Fours are the shoppers of the Enneagram, often with vast wardrobes and nothing to wear. If their partner is shopping for clothes, they may feel panic that there isn't enough money, and then the urge to buy themselves something right away before the money is gone.

When Sexual Fours are in an open relationship, they will usually need to have more lovers more often than their partner does. This competition, on a deeper level, is actually directed at their rivals — members of their own sex, whom they would wish away, if they could.

On the analytic side of the dichotomy, Sexual Fours present themselves as sharp and opinionated. Jimi Hendrix and Marlon Brando are examples of the unique style of the Sexual Four.

Additional Exemplars

An excellent film was made about the life of Japanese novelist Yukio Mishima, a Self-preservation Four who lived his life as theater: *A Life in Four Chapters*. Raised by women and longing for the father he never had, Mishima persevered. A novelist and political adventurer, he created his own private army in Japan. The uniforms of the army were exquisite. Mishima used Japanese society as a giant stage for playing out the melodrama of his life. He staged a takeover of parliament by his army to publicize his romantic notions, calling for a return to a sacred samurai culture. He longed for the days of chivalry and knighthood as a way of attaining the purity of the Japanese spirit. His behind-the-scenes kinky sex and self-mutilation reflected the Four's manifestation of the dark hidden scar. He ended his life by staging his own suicide as a public media event.

This Boy's Life, starring Leonardo DiCaprio, is an excellent film about the relationship between a teenage male Four, his Eight step-father, Robert De Niro, and Two mother, Ellen Barkin.

Charlie Chaplin is an example of the Sexual Four. Playing the sad, lovable little tramp, Chaplin ruined his own life in the pursuit of young women. The film *Chaplin* is a beautiful portrayal by an actor of the same fixation, Robert Downey Jr.

The following poem by R.D. Laing perfectly illustrates the Four's longing to be loved and the endless cycle of searching outside themselves for confirmation of self-worth.

Do You Love Me?

by R.D. Laing

She: Do you love me? *He*: Yes, I love you. *She*: Best of all? *He*: Yes, best of all. *She*: More than the whole world? *He*: Yes, more than the whole world. *She*: Do you like me?

He: Yes, I like you. *She*: Do you like being near me? *He*: Yes, I like being near you.

She: Do you like to look at me? *He*: Yes, I like to look at you. *She*: Do you think I'm stupid? *He*: No, I don't think you're stupid. *She*: Do you think I'm attractive? *He*: Yes, I think you're attractive. *She*: Do I bore you?

He: No, you don't bore me. *She*: Do you like my eyebrows? *He*: Yes, I like your eyebrows. *She*: Very much? *He*: Very much. *She*: Which one do you like the most? *He*: If I say one, the other will be jealous. *She*: You have to say. *He*: They are both exquisite. *She*: Honest? *He*: Honest. *She*: Do I have nice eyelashes? *He*: Yes, nice eyelashes. *She*: Do you like to smell me? *He*: Yes, I like to smell you. *She*: Do you like my perfume? *He*: Yes, I like your perfume. *She*: Do you think I've good taste? *He*: Yes, you have good taste. *She*: Do you think I am talented? *He*: Yes, I think you're talented. *She*: You don't think I'm lazy? *He*: No, I don't think you're lazy. *She*: Do you like to touch me? *He*: Yes, I like to touch you. *She*: Do you think I am funny? *He*: Only in a nice way. *She*: Are you laughing at me?

He: No, I'm not laughing at you. *She*: Do you really love me? *He*: Yes, I really love you. *She*: Say, "I love you."

He: I love you. *She*: Do you want to hug me? *He*: Yes, I want to hug you, and cuddle you, and bill and coo with you. *She*: Is it all right? *He*: Yes, it is all right. *She*: Swear you will never leave me. *He*: I swear I'll never leave you, cross my heart and hope to die if I tell a lie.

(pause) *She*: Do you really love me?

Exemplars by Subtype

Self-Preservation~Dauntless:

Bette Davis, Steve Martin, Tim Burton, Teri Garr, Paul Simon, Michael Keaton, Roberta Flack, Peter Lorre, Edith Piaf, Scarlett O'Hara, Sammy Davis Jr., Jack Lemmon, Japan

Social~Shame:

Judy Garland, Buster Keaton, Kate Wolf, Neil Young, Cat Stevens, Bobby "Blue" Bland, Leonard Cohen, Marisa Tomei, Keane paintings, Jackie Gleason, San Francisco gay culture

Sexual~Competition:

Jimi Hendrix, Tupac Shakur, Marlon Brando, Johnny Depp, Amy Winehouse, Kevin Durant, Ingrid Bergman, Charlie Chaplin, Michelle Pfeiffer, Val Kilmer, Willem Dafoe, Robert Downey Jr., Billie Holiday, Van Morrison, Miles Davis, John Coltrane, Simone de Beauvoir, Madame Bovary, Yukio Mishima, Italy

Paranoid Schizophrenics:

The Fear Points

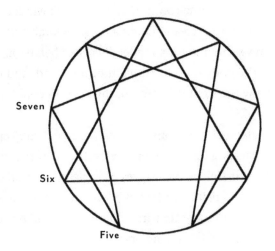

When you experience your fear, you become fearless.
All other fears merge with that fear.
If you fear that fear, then you will become fearful.
Be fearless, all your fears will flee.

— Kabir

In the fear points, the fixation is crystallized in the mental body. Empty intelligence is veiled by the chattering mind that calls itself intelligent. These are people who have a fear of fear. Living in the mind is a way of avoiding the emotion of fear. These points then use their minds as a form of protection against what is perceived as a threatening world. As a style, the fear points move away from people. Sometimes called the "doing" group, these people are always dealing with a strong polarity between doing and trying to decide what to do. This is also the home of internal dialogue. All fixations have internal dialogue, but the fear points — in particular, the Sixes — are especially addicted. Their powerful absorption with inner ideas or objects tends to prevent them from taking clear, decisive action.

Sixes hide behind belief systems as a way of avoiding primal instincts. In this way they lose connection with their own deep instinctive sense. This in turn creates doubt and behavioral stuttering.

Sixes are always searching for a model of correct behavior. The sense is that the body is an instrument of the mind, and if the mind just knew the right thing to do, then action could flow effortlessly.

Sevens make lateral connections between unrelated subjects in order to create a dazzling display of virtuosity. In this way they distract the listener as well as themselves from deep emotional contact and thus avoid pain. Terrified of being present in the moment, Sevens overcompensate with endless plans and options which they may perceive as "staying open to God's will."

Fives collect information and knowledge as a protection against the perceived threat of being overwhelmed by the outside world or falling into the black hole of the inside world. Feeling coerced by outside relationships, they retreat into an inner mental world.

Point Six: The Core Fear Point

Essence:	Emptiness, Pure Intelligence
Holy Idea:	Trust
Holy Path:	Courage
Chief Feature:	Paranoia
Passion:	Doubt
Idealization:	"I am loyal"
Talking Style:	Setting limits
Trap:	Security
Defense Mechanism:	Projection
Avoidance:	Deviance
Dichotomy:	Pushy/Surrender
Subtypes:	Self-Preservation~Warmth Social~Duty Sexual~Strength/Beauty

Six is the core fear point. Just as we find an apparent absence of anger in the core anger point and an apparent absence of hysteria in the core hysteric point, we also find an apparent absence of fear in the core fear point. Sixes are the point on the Enneagram most dissociated from the emotion of fear. Unexperienced, frozen terror compels the Six to adopt strategies that create a perception of safety.

Sixes live in the mental body as a way of avoiding fear. This is the home of psychology and cold logic. This is the place of chess players, philosophers, and internal dialogue. Descartes' famous dictum, "I think, therefore I am," (Cogito, Ergo Sum) epitomizes the Six fixation. Sixes are always trying to figure out the world in their head, carrying on nonstop conversations with themselves, and continuously running a commentary about what is being experienced.

Because they live in the mind, Sixes lose contact with the emotions and the body, which leads to uncertainty and doubt. The issue for Sixes is movement into action; there are usually a thousand head trips between the idea and acting it out.

In order to appreciate the state that Sixes live in, imagine that you are sleeping in a house out in the country on a stormy night. You are upstairs in the bedroom, and you are all alone. Suddenly, you awaken from your sleep because you think you heard a sound. You are not sure if you really heard it or not. You lie in bed, holding your breath, listening, hyper-alert to every sound. As you try to listen this voice in your head is shouting, "Did I hear it or was it my imagination? Be quiet, I can't hear. What was that? Was that just my mind? Is there really someone down there? Oh, shut up so I can think!"

This approximates the condition of the Six. Ever-vigilant for the coming threat, just waiting for the next shoe to drop, Sixes have difficulties with exhaustion and action. When the other shoe does drop, when the sound downstairs is confirmed, they can move into action. Once the danger is real and has been defined, the Six becomes the hero. Thus, we find Sixes who are ambulance drivers, hospital emergency room workers, policemen, and professional athletes.

When there is no present danger and no organizational structure to which the Six is loyal, we see a life pattern of behavioral stutterings. False starts and stops can plague a Six's life. I had a Six client who went through three masters' programs but never wrote the thesis for any of them. Sixes often stop careers in midstream and decide to try something else.

Sixes use loyalty to an organization as a way of avoiding false starts and stops. The military, the police, and team sports are natural homes for Sixes. Loyalty and duty to the organization will keep them functioning. A Six who was a successful small businessman went to work six days a week for thirty years out of a sense of duty to his family, and loyalty to his organization. It helped that his father, an Eight, was his partner in the business.

While organizations and structure can keep the Six functioning, authority in general is viewed as incompetent. Despite this view, Sixes are afraid to push authority too hard. The fear is that if the structure is pushed too hard it will crumble and lead to chaos. This is Freud's fear of the id, symbolically a hulking, hairy, polymorphous, perverse beast of the depths, that must be kept locked up by the ego. Thus, you find Sixes continually nitpicking at authority. They will gossip and talk behind the authority's back, but rarely engage in direct confrontation unless they feel safe. Sixes enjoy a clear pecking order, which is also a reflection of the internal order needed to control the feared primal urges.

Since they view the body as an instrument of the mind, many Sixes become professional athletes. Often the physical discharge of sports will drain off some of their paranoid energy. They may be runners addicted to their running, or black belts in karate. In martial arts and other professional sports, the area of combat is clearly delineated, which allows them to focus and perform.

Freud was a Six, and all of Freudian psychology may be said to be the structure of a male Six analyzing hysteric females. Sixes love to understand, and in particular are fascinated with the mind and how it works. There can also be an attraction or fascination with madness and what is beyond the mind. Sixes often visit psychiatric wards, or work as psychiatrists, as a way to safely view the madness and chaos lurking just beyond the logical boundaries of an ordered mind.

Because Sixes are always scanning for the threat, they can be excellent observers. Sixes tend to look behind the scenes to pick up the real meaning. They do not ignore or overlook the information in front of them; rather, they look for the meaning behind what is apparent. Scanning for danger has also developed their psychic ability. Every professional psychic I have ever met has been a Six.

The great tragedy of the Six fixation is the deep terror of being alone, which is covered by the strongly held idea of false independence and the sense that "I have to do it myself." This masks the Six's almost bottomless fear of believing herself to be incompetent, of not knowing what to do, and therefore being abandoned. Many Sixes have reported the fear of falling into a black hole and drifting in space without knowing what to do, having no contact, and feeling completely abandoned by God. This primal fear is then used by the Six mind to misidentify as a Four fixation. The difference is that the Six's issue is not about abandonment, but rather the *fear* of abandonment.

In the belief, "I have to do it myself," I have seen many Sixes turn their back on genuine help. They often congregate in workshops and in various spiritual communities. Yet, I have seen many Sixes, after sitting with the Master and having their minds stop through the grace of the guru's transmission, get up and walk out, never to return, because "I have to do it myself."

Passion: Doubt

The passion that runs the Six machine is *doubt*. They doubt everything. Doubt manifests first in internal dialogue, as they doubt both themselves and the world. After learning something about the Enneagram, most Sixes doubt that they are Sixes. First, they rebel against the thought of being put into a confining box of a system. They don't like to be classified, they explain. After deciding to give the system a chance to prove itself, most Sixes are quickly sure that they are not Sixes, for in truth they are much more aware of their anger or their sadness, rather than their fear.

Self-preservation Sixes may be more aware of their desire to help others than of their experience of fear. Thus, many Self-preservation Sixes will classify themselves as Twos. Others will think of themselves as Fours, Sevens, Fives, or Eights. When asked for a deep emotion, they will often say, "I think I am feeling . . ." or, "I feel confused." Confusion, of course, is a mental state, not an emotional one. This distinction is often virgin territory for the doubting mind.

The passion of doubt manifests in the Six's belief that there is a hidden meaning behind what is apparent. By constantly looking for the hidden, they doubt the obvious. A Six may outwardly appear to agree with you, while secretly doubting your motives.

Doubt also manifests in an inability to get started. Procrastination in the Six is the playing out of Hamlet's dilemma, "To be or not to be." Sixes doubt their own abilities and whether any choice they make is the correct one. Then they doubt the doubts.

Because they are living in the mental realm where anything and everything is possible, there is a lack of ground for reality checking. Instead of getting a "gut feeling" and acting on it, Sixes avoid gut feelings as a way of avoiding both fear and the possible deviance of the primal urges.

Childhood Setting

Sixes frequently had an incompetent parent, usually the father. Their father may have been an alcoholic, a failure in business, or simply absent from the family. One Six described her father going bankrupt at his donut business when she was six years old. She went to work babysitting to help take care of the family. Yet no one outside of the immediate family was allowed to know this family secret.

Sixes often describe being four or five years old and having to take care of Mommy. They often feel that they were cast into the role of adult long before they were ready. The feeling of incompetence becomes the root of their doubt. Having an incompetent father later manifests as the Six's distrust of the competency of authority. All this leads Sixes to doubt themselves and the world, and to believe that things are not what they appear to be. It also leads to a lifetime of looking for heroes, then knocking them off the pedestal. Feeling betrayed by their father, Sixes become addicted to continual self-betrayal projected out as betrayal by the other. This perceived betrayal by others becomes the justification for betraying others in the safety of secrecy and alliances, and in the name of truth and decency.

Sixes often report that in childhood there was a family secret. It might have been that Mom was an alcoholic or that one of the kids was adopted.

The Six whose father went bankrupt moved to another town and told everyone that Dad sold his old business in order to move here. This family secret creates a war-zone mentality. There is a tight bonding in the loyalty of the family, and a constant alertness to make sure that no one outside the group finds out. This crystallizes as the Six's idealization of loyalty. In the name of loyalty there is often self-betrayal projected out as the betrayal of the father.

In the Self-preservation Six, we often find that actual issues of survival manifested in infancy. One Self-preservation Six reported that she was asthmatic and came close to death in infancy. Another almost strangled in the crib. In reliving the memory, he felt that there was no one there competent to help, and he had to scream for help to ensure his own survival.

Another Self-preservation Six describes the feeling of danger whenever his alcoholic Eight father was in a bad mood:

I remember being punished almost randomly. Punishment was more dependent on my father's moods than on my behaviors. I felt terrified of him when he was angry and was never sure what I had to do to stay "out of trouble." I had to learn how to be sensitive to his moods. I knew when it was the right time to ask him for something I wanted and when it was time to make myself invisible. When I was younger, he spent most of his time at work or in bars. When he was home, sometimes he was warm, loving, and fun to be with. At other times he was like a time bomb ready to explode at one of us. When he was in a bad mood, we all had to be quiet and stay out of his way. If I were to be heard playing, fighting, or laughing, this could set his anger off. I remember fearing that he would kill me if I ever crossed him. My mother later agreed that this was a possibility.

In the Sexual Six, we sometimes find deep trauma in the birth process. Sexual Sixes often report having dangerous or bloody births, where blood, sex, birth, and death are all present in a terrifying knot. Thus, there can be a deep terror around any of these issues.

In the childhood of most Sixes, the bogeymen lurked in the closet. They scare themselves with their own thoughts and nightmares. These children then make judgments about themselves and their ability to hurt someone with their thoughts. This process keeps the bad thoughts out of their consciousness. However, it creates a haunting of the subconscious that further inhibits their ability to act.

Idealization: "I am loyal."

The idealization of the Six is, "I am loyal." This begins at a very early age in the context of the family. This loyalty to the family often stays with Sixes throughout their lives. The loyalty also gets transferred to other groups or organizations. Sixes are team players. The feeling is "If we all do our jobs together, we can get through this alive." The feeling of sharing a foxhole in a war zone creates a deep bonding of loyalty in the Six.

Marine Colonel Oliver North was a loyal Six in service to President Reagan. North was the hero gladly "taking spears in the chest" in protection of his commander-in-chief. Thus, North protected the President's illegal activities by claiming full responsibility for selling weapons to Iran and supplying the terrorists in Nicaragua.

The flip side of this is the issue of betrayal. Sixes stay loyal as long as there is a perceived sense of group loyalty. Once they believe they have been betrayed by the group, however, they can justify betrayal in kind. And so, Oliver North began to talk.

Talking Style: Setting Limits

The talking style of the Six is called *setting limits*. This means keeping things manageable. The grandiose thinking of an Eight, for example, will be countered by the Six's desire to keep things in manageable proportions.

Woody Allen always spoke about keeping his projects low budget. He loves using just one apartment as the set. He feels that by keeping a project small, even if it fails to make money, the studio will let him do another one.

One way setting limits can manifest in the Six talking style is by searching for the right thing to do in order to avoid making a mistake, which could lead to criticism or attack. In the quotation below, a Six illustrates how setting limits as a talking style can be a way of finding out what the rules of the game are, in order to avoid the perceived danger of going beyond the bounds of what is expected from others:

In my relationships with people, I feel a need to be "clear" in all my communication. Being clear means that I understand what you want or expect from me, and I have made my feelings and intentions known. There is a sense of making sure that I have communicated to everyone whatever I may need to so that my ass is covered. I want to ensure that I am not going to be the target of someone's anger, criticism, or disappointment.

There is this sense of not knowing what behavior is appropriate and wanting to know what the rules are, the parameters, the limits within which I am safe. It's felt as a need to communicate clearly in order to find out how I should be and what I should do or not do so that I don't get into any trouble.

The distrust of authority — usually stemming from childhood feelings that their parents were not competent enough to take care of them — may express itself in the talking style of the Six as testing whoever is in the place of power. The bumper sticker, "Question Authority," is a Six slogan.

One Six said:

I see myself as being pushy against authority, but not to any extreme because then I would have doubts about the other extremists I'm with. If they are loyal and I can have set limits, then I can go for it. But I don't want to be subject to this craziness. I need to know where I am going.

Another Six shared that she wouldn't question or challenge the authority directly, but would attack the power by sharing her criticisms with people she thought would be in agreement with her. Her outspoken challenge of the authority behind the scenes gave her a sense that she was the one who was really in power. She also added that to confront the authority directly would be terrifying. Some Sixes are more willing to be more confrontational than others, but all Sixes want to stay within the limits that feel safe to them.

The Trap: Security

The trap of the Six is *security*. Sixes will sell out their adventures into the unknown by staying safe within the current structure. When the idea of risk appears, security becomes the test to determine whether action will be taken. This, in turn, leads to doubt and vacillation.

Security for the Six is knowing there are limits to the risks, or parameters to the action being contemplated. Knowing the options and possible consequences beforehand also creates a sense of security. This, however, requires knowing the future, which invariably leads to doubt. One Six said, "I must feel secure before

I can move at all." Since security is based on a future projection of the mind cut off from instinctive nature, every possible situation is projected, examined, doubted, and re-thought. This leads to a paralysis of action.

Since insecurity leads to fear, and fear is avoided by thought, whenever issues of security arise (and this may be all the time) the mind starts racing. This is a strategy to avoid the fear of the unknown.

One Six reported having the realization that every decision she had ever made in her entire life had been based on fear.

A word that comes up a lot in the Six vocabulary is "interesting." This is a noncommittal, mentally disassociated comment that hides the Six's true opinion as a way to stay safe and in rapport.

Defense Mechanism: Projection

The defense mechanism in the Six is called *projection*. The movie, *The Treasure of Sierra Madre*, gives an excellent example of this. Bogart plays a down-and-out bum in Mexico who discovers gold in the Sierra Madre. Feeling greed for the gold, Bogart's character becomes paranoid by projecting his greed onto the others. He then betrays his comrades, feeling justified because he has projected the betrayal onto them. The scene of him coming down the mountain talking to himself is a classic portrayal of a Six gone off the deep end.

To compensate for feelings of fear and distrust, Sixes may project hostile motives onto those around them. Because they are always doubting and looking for hidden meaning behind the scenes, there is a tendency to project hidden motives onto the behavior of others. A Six who has a crush on the boss's secretary might muse, "Why do you suppose he really gave me that raise? It could be because he has a crush on his secretary and wants to get me out of the way."

Often the father is projected onto figures of authority. Sixes may subconsciously rebel against their father by betraying their boss.

Avoidance: Deviance

Sixes avoid *deviance*. There is a deep fear of the polymorphous, perverse Id. The primal energy of sexuality is thought of as an un- predictable savage force, which, if ever allowed to manifest freely, may become deviant. This fear and the resulting movement into the mind are clearly described in a dream that was shared by a Six:

I came to a very big house. It was very large and modern inside. In the house I met people known and unknown to me. I was to sleep in a side room that was older. It had a stairway leading down to a base- ment. I felt fear as I passed the stairway. Fear of something down there. I believed it was something dark and unwholesome. Then I slept in this side room. Soon I awoke terrified and feeling possessed by what was in the cellar. It had come into my body. I felt frozen with terror and unable to move or call out. Something alien and unwholesome seemed to be controlling my body.

I said, "NO" strongly and repeatedly to this that was possessing my body. I thought that this was something outside, negative, and evil, and it must not be allowed to have possession. It was strange. For several moments my body was frozen and my face contorted like a monster's as I said, "NO."

Then I went away from this old part of the house, looking for a safe place to spend the night, or someone to help me understand this that I was so afraid of. I wanted to go back there with them and see what it was. I was too afraid to be alone.

As I entered this large house, the open-style room was as big as a barn. On the wall, there were hundreds of light switches. I did not know which switch to turn on. I tried a few until I got some light in the room. I then went upstairs and found a heavily padded door that led to a music room. It was like a central headquarters. There I found a friend amidst a vast array of musical equipment, computers, etc. I thought this room would be safe. It overlooked the big room of barn-like house and had a window you could look down through.

Suddenly, "IT" grabbed my body and began to wrestle my body toward the window, intending to push me through it.

As a counter to fear, Sixes sometimes display a forced bravado and machismo. This is exemplified in "Miller time" commercials, in which the men stand around the bar telling dirty jokes, crushing beer cans with their hands, and spitting on the floor. Sixes need to prove their manhood, as many do in the roles of motorcycle cops and drill sergeants.

Spanish culture, with its bullfights and flamenco, stiletto heels and knives, gives the flavor of the Sexual Six machismo, tinged with dangerous sexuality.

One female Six, a grade school art teacher, told me she felt that if she ever really let her sexuality out she would become a whore. Therefore, she only had affairs with married men, which seemed safe to her.

Since deep primal emotions are avoided as a way of avoiding fear and deviance, Sixes occasionally have issues of erratic erections or difficulties with orgasm. These conditions are also related to the dissociative effects of internal dialogue. Sex is seen as a performance, with the mind as the observer and commentator. This becomes magnified in the Sexual Six, where sex is a performance and a betrayal. Madonna's Catholic schoolgirl pornography is a good example of this performance being acted out to the extreme.

The Dichotomy: Pushy/Surrender

The dichotomy is called *pushy/surrender*. Both styles represent strategies for dealing with threat. The pushy Six may act confrontational and belligerent as a stance to ward off threat. The outward appearance might be a scowling, hostile, belligerent stance toward strangers. Yet this easily collapses into surrender in the face of authority.

The German culture is a Six, and its stance is that of the pushy Six. The military and police are also examples of the pushy Six style. The paranoia of lurking danger is dealt with by a machismo bravado. The black belt karate champion who saunters through tough neighborhoods also exemplifies this style.

The surrender Six, on the other hand, is interested in making alliances in order to deflect threat. Many Self-preservation Sixes are surrender Sixes. There is a sense of harmlessness, along with offers of loyalty and cooperation, in order to deflect attack. Although one side of the dichotomy will be prominent, the flip side is just in the background, waiting for the right opportunity to be expressed. One Six describes this play of the dichotomy:

I have become aware of how at times I will be pushy and author-itative, and at other times I will be more passive and submissive. It depends upon whether I think I am safe or not. If I think I am really safe and that the other person I am dealing with is on the weak side, then I may be pushier. But if I think the other person is stronger, I will surren-der. And that happens very intuitively. But I notice in certain group situ-ations that I'll be really, really pushy. In my primary relationship, which is with a Six, we constantly do this flip of who's in the role of pushy and who's in the role of surrender. Both responses happen when there is fear and a sense that I have to protect myself in some way. Both are a form of control, to defend against losing control.

Subtypes

Self-Preservation: Warmth

Self-preservation Sixes are *warm*, caring people who deflect the threat or danger by being helpful. Sometimes compared to a harm-less rabbit, the warm Six is a people-helper. Woody Allen person-ifies this subtype. A sense of warm caring pervades the style and mood of his movies.

A man who was a participant in an Enneagram retreat describes this style of the Six as it can manifest in the realm of relationships:

I perceive survival as the need to make the environment non-threatening by avoiding power. Alliances are made with those perceived to be non-threatening and of the same power. Alliances with those who are more powerful are not perceived to be as safe because there is an underlying distrust of those who have power. Alliances with those of less power are not perceived to be as safe because there is the danger of becoming the authority figure and attacked and rebelled against. Autonomy and self-reliance are prized. There is an unwillingness to allow anybody to have power over me, as there is also an unwillingness to overpower anybody else.

Pre-Holocaust European Jewry was a warm Six culture. The terror of survival was dealt with by appearing harmless and living in the head, with endless discussion and arguments. With a love of learning and the intellect, the traditional European Jewish style is to study and debate abstract ideas all day. Paranoid (perhaps rightfully so), the style is the surrender side of the dichotomy, to appear safe and non-threatening in order to deflect attack. The pushiness appears in the safety of family relationships. Anxiety is usually projected onto significant others.

For the most part, the warm Sixes of Europe didn't leave for the unknown of the Promised Land--and perished in the ovens. This is quite different from modern-day Israel, which is an Eight culture, founded by pioneers, and led by terrorists against the British.

Quite often, I find female therapists to be Self-preservation Sixes. Therapy is a safe place to expose emotions, allowing them to be people-helpers and indulging their fascination with the mind.

Initially, warm Sixes often misidentify themselves as Twos. In general, however, they are more nervous than Twos, and the motivation is not seduction but safety. The selfless Jewish mother, often identified as a Two, can be a warm Six in disguise.

Some warm Sixes identify themselves as Nines because they avoid conflict and anger. But while the motivation of the Nine is the fear of killing someone, the motivation of the Six is the fear of being killed.

Social: Duty

The duty Six is the home of the motorcycle cop. There is often a dry-brushed look to the grooming, with a short-clipped mustache and neatly trimmed hair, sometimes resembling the helmet look found in the One. Duty is the paramount force that drives life. There is always a strong sense of duty to the family, even when it is consciously rebelled against.

One female Social Six reported that she never had lovers who weren't married. She was afraid that if she ever married and had children, her sense of duty would destroy her career.

Duty Sixes are almost always involved with their parents, and conflict with parental authority continues late into life. Middle-aged duty Sixes may still fight with their parents about coming "home" for Christmas. They most always "do their duty," whether they like it or not.

A good diagnostic for the Social Six is the question: "Did you go home for Christmas?" The answer may be, "Yes," or, "No, not this year," or, "I hate going home," or, "I always go home for Christmas," but "home" is always immediately perceived as being where the parents live.

Hamlet is a Social Six. Paralyzed by doubt, the play revolves around his inability to take action against his father's killer, who is now sleeping with his mother.

One Social Six I know is in his seventies and now retired. He worked methodically his whole life, rarely missing a day of work, out of a sense of duty to his family. His father, now in his nineties, is still alive. They fight constantly. The son continues to play out the role of dutiful son and continues to be verbally abused by his Eight father. Yet this doesn't stop him from calling every day and visiting several times a week.

One male Six was doubtful that Six was his fixation, because he ran away from home at eighteen and never looked back. Upon investigation, it turned out that he joined the Green Berets, who became his family for the next thirty years.

Sexual: Strength and Beauty

Strength and beauty Sixes are always either *strong* and/or *beautiful*. They then make alliances with other strong or beautiful partners. Some Sexual Sixes, always outwardly pushy rather than surrendered, are counterphobic (attracted to the very danger they fear). Not all Sexual Sixes are counterphobic, but most counterphobic Sixes are of the Sexual subtype. Thus, we find that many skydivers, mountain climbers, and stunt men fall into this category.

Evel Kneivel was once perhaps the best known counterphobic Six in our culture. He made his reputation and living by doing crazy, death-defying stunts. After trying unsuccessfully to use his motorcycle to leap across a canyon gorge — and almost dying in the attempt — he tried it again. He has been shot from cannons and has suffered innumerable broken bones. Despite breaking his neck, his spine, and every other part of his body, he was drawn to continue.

Spain is a Sexual Six culture. Bullfighting is a classic Sexual Six activity where a beautiful man in tight pants faces death with a cape and a sword. An Eight, by contrast, would just shoot the bull.

A famous female bullfighter in Spain is a Sexual Six. In an interview, she said that as a child she knew if she didn't make it as a bullfighter, she would become either a firefighter or police officer.

Flamenco dancing, with its castanets, puffy shoulders, and stomping heels, is also the flavor of Sexual Six, as are the black leather and switchblades of the machismo culture.

A Sexual Six in one of my workshops was a ski instructor. He claimed to be stronger than any of the men in the room. He said he could do death-defying feats on skis, but he was terrified of approaching a woman and asking for a date.

Sylvester Stallone and Brigitte Nielson were a wonderful example of a strength-and-beauty couple. Sexual Sixes may think of themselves as Eights, and Stallone may portray Eights in his movies, but it is usually the Sexual Six who works on the body and becomes a weightlifter, bodybuilder type. The paunch of Jack Nicholson or the body of Robert De Niro, both Eights, is very different from the beautiful muscular body of Arnold Schwarzenegger, a Sexual Six.

Strength-and-beauty Sixes are sometimes the hardest to spot on the Enneagram. Many people adopt styles of different fixations and at first might not recognize their point on the Enneagram. Nines who live in motorcycle gangs are an example.

Sexual Sixes, however, have adopted the most disguises to avoid dealing with the terror associated with sex and death. One Sexual Six I know is certain she is a Two. She considers herself a people-helper and is outraged by the suggestion that she's a Six. Another Sexual Six started therapy thinking she was a Four. She was an artist — a feeling, melancholy, moody person — not a Six, she proclaimed, and dozens of others. So many in fact that we have a special category for "Sixes who think they are Fours."

Male Sexual Sixes sometimes regard themselves as macho Eights. One male Sexual Six, a black belt Aikido instructor, is certain he is a Seven. Of any fixation, the hardest to identify is the male beauty Six. The male Sexual Six who is on the surrender side of the dichotomy is often a beauty Six rather than a strength Six. He therefore may look like a cross between a Four and a Seven, dressing like a Four but windsurfing like a Seven. The Maui spiritual community is peopled with Sevens and beauty Sexual Sixes. Osho (Bhagwan Shree Rajneesh,) was a beauty Sexual Six, dressing like a four and proclaiming a Seven philosophy that eroticism, sex, dance, and group living can lead to Enlightenment.

Additional Exemplars

Interestingly enough, both German and Jewish cultures are Six cultures. Germany represents the pushy Social Six. Duty to the family and the recognition of duty to the "fatherland" is a Germanic stance. Walking down the street, Germans avoid eye contact. There is a scowling fierceness to their social mask. The German beer hall is a very Social Six-ish phenomenon. Of course, the German language itself is the language of science and logic. Hitler's appeal rested on the paranoid threats from "outside" and "other" that threatened the fatherland. There was a strong sexual projection as well, as Hitler worried about the deflowering of German womanhood by the dark and evil Jews, which represent the id in the basement.

Angela Merkel, the current head of Germany, exemplifies the cultural and psychic shift of the population that the leader is now a woman. As a Social Six she was involved in the church in East Germany and is a family and community person. She is stolid and sensible with a Social Six hairdo and bulldog demeanor. She is a leader that works well with others, has phased out nuclear power and is transitioning her country to a green future. She is among the best of what's left of the western world's leaders, as the US reels under Donald Trump.

Dan White is perhaps a classic example of the psychotic break that can happen in Sixes. He was a fireman and then a policeman after serving in the military. A Social Six, he ran successfully for county supervisor in San Francisco. After some time, he resigned his seat because he couldn't make enough money to support his family.

Almost immediately after White's resignation, the late Mayor Moscone appointed the first openly gay politician to fill his seat. This triggered White on a deep subconscious level. He tried to withdraw his resignation and demanded his seat back. When he didn't get what he wanted, he went to the city hall and shot and killed the mayor and Harvey Milk, the man appointed to replace him. His defense was that eating Twinkies gave him a sugar rush and made him crazy.

Jim Jones, a Social Six, was the leader of a working-class social movement through his church. After years of good work in the community, he ended up taking his flock into the jungles of

Guyana in Central America. He became increasingly paranoid; first, that the government of Guyana was out to get him, and then that the American government was as well. When the United States sent Congressman John Ryan to investigate, Ryan was shot and killed. Jones and almost the entire church then committed ritual suicide together.

David Koresh, a messianic Christian figure to his followers, was a Six with paranoid delusions of grandeur. A cult developed around him, and they armed themselves for the coming Armageddon. Almost all of them died in a fiery shoot-out with government agents at their church compound in Waco, Texas.

The Marlboro man exemplifies the Six bravado. Steve McQueen also represents the Six style. George Lucas, the director of the *Star Wars* trilogy, is an example of a successful Social Six. In a recent interview he speaks of "reigning in" the emotionality of Francis Ford Coppola, of setting limits and timelines. His *Star Wars* films are the classic embodiment of the Six hero. A boy without a father who goes off in search of adventure. A father figure teaches him to trust "the force," fight the dark side, and discover that his father is the betraying villain who must be destroyed for the good of civilization.

Bare-chested Vladimir Putin, the black-belt judo practitioner and ex-KGB agent is a Sexual Six. He is not the usual blustering Eight of Kruschev, Brezhnev or Boris Yeltsin. He is more like a Doberman Pinscher: sleek and scary and attacks without barking first.

I had a Sexual Six client whose story illustrates the Sexual Six fixation well. When she was five years old, she had a crush on her Eight father, and he was also attracted to her. He was a photographer who spent a lot of time in his darkroom, where she was not allowed. One day she snuck in and discovered her father's Playboy magazines. The symbolic richness of sneaking into her father's "dark room" and finding pictures of naked women impressed itself on her in a very deep way. She became extremely attracted/repulsed and ultimately terrified by the pictures.

Soon after, she had a dream in which she was sitting at the kitchen table late at night (something she said she would never do as a five-year-old). As she sat there, the "bogeyman" came out of her father's darkroom wielding a big knife. He looked at her and said, "I'm going upstairs to kill your parents. When I am done, I am going to come down and kill you."

As the bogeyman started walking up the stairs, she tried to hide by pretending that she was reading the newspaper, though she was too young to read. She was so frozen in terror that she did not cry out to warn her parents. That moment of being frozen, of being so terrified that movement is impossible, crystallized the fixation. From then on, she felt deeply guilty, due both to her inability to act, and the possibility of what was lurking just beneath the surface of her conscious mind.

Exemplars by Subtype

Self-Preservation~Warmth:

Woody Allen, Spike Lee, Julia Louis-Dreyfus, Dick Cavett, Gilda Radner, Billy Crystal, worrying, bicycling, European Jewish culture

Social~Duty:

Luke Skywalker, Adolf Hitler, George Lucas, Confucius, Hamlet, Oliver North, William Buckley, Dan White, Janet Reno, Bill Moyers, Angela Merkel, firemen, motorcycle police, football linemen, PTA (Parent Teacher Association), Germany

Sexual~Strength/Beauty:

Cher, Madonna, Lady Gaga, Angelina Jolie, Sylvester Stallone, Bruce Willis, Katy Perry, Beyoncé, Kim Kardashian, Mel Gibson, Brigitte Nielson, Britney Spears, Demi Moore, Julianne Moore, Arnold Schwarzenegger, Evel Knievel, Steve McQueen, Kirk Douglas, Ursula Andress, Sigourney Weaver, Jamie Lee Curtis, Gloria Steinem, Dennis

*Rodman, Sigmund Freud, Osho Rajneesh, Vladimir Putin, bullfighting,
skydivers, bungee-cord jumpers, Spain*

Point Seven: The Exteriorized Fear Point

Essence:	Absorption
Holy Idea:	Holy Work
Holy Path:	Sobriety
Chief Feature:	Planning
Passion:	Gluttony
Idealization:	"I am okay"
Talking Style:	Stories
Trap:	Idealist
Defense Mechanism:	Rationalization
Avoidance:	Pain
Dichotomy:	Inferior/Superior
Subtypes:	Self-Preservation~Extended Family Social~Martyr Sexual~Suggestibility

Seven is the externalized fear point. These are the charmers, con artists, and cosmic travelers of the Enneagram. For the Seven, searching on the outside for the new and the different veils the essence of inner absorption.

This is the home of magical thinking. Sevens believe that if we all think enough good thoughts, everything will turn out in the end. "Don't bring me down" is the Seven commandment. One Seven describes this really well in the following story:

I always felt I could do anything I wanted. When I was about six or seven, I wanted to fly. I got up on the garage and was just ready to take off, when I thought it might be a good idea to go down and make a little pile of pine needles, just in case the first time didn't work.

And so I went down and made a big pile, and then I went back up. I knew that if I really believed it, I could do it. I just leapt off as if I was on a hang glider. And I was really shocked that I fell. Then I thought that the reason I fell was because I had made the pile, and if I hadn't made the pile, I wouldn't have fallen.

Peter Pan is the quintessential Seven. Peter Pan taught the Darling children that they could fly by thinking good thoughts. "Think of candy, and you are almost there . . . Christmas is lift-off!"

Sevens will come into your life to cheer you up. They may tell you an entertaining story when you take them out to dinner, "singing for their supper" so to speak. They might make love with you in order to enlighten you, and then move on.

This is the place of new ideas and New Age thinking. LSD, communal living, and walking barefoot in the streets with flowers in your hair--all have the flavor of Seven. Sevens were into health food before the rest of us. Cary Grant was doing LSD and drinking carrot juice in the 1950s. Gypsy Boots was a Seven troubadour in the 1950s who had his own line of health foods and dietary fiber.

Sevens love to skate on new ideas. This is a place of synthetic, or associative, thinking. They love to bring together new and interesting combinations. But they do not like to be "brought down" by discussions of last night's new idea, or by staying with a single thought to give it depth.

These are the future thinkers. For them, the present is made tolerable by the future. Sevens always envision us moving into a Golden Age. Things are going to get better.

Passion: Gluttony

The passion that runs the Seven machine is called *gluttony*. This is not necessarily gluttony for food, but gluttony for experience. A Seven who spent the whole night partying and is now sleeping it off probably feels a little worried that he is missing something.

When eating in a restaurant, the Seven prefers a buffet smorgasbord; to choose from the menu can be an ordeal. Once the choice is made, there is often the letdown of noticing what wasn't chosen.

Ultimately, regardless of fixation, there is only one true choice. This is the choice to be free from the bondage of identifying oneself as a body with a particular style of fixation. In the willingness to turn away from phenomena — renouncing the search for happiness in phenomenal experience — freedom is realized to be one's present and prior condition. Making this final and true choice, which is the same as surrender, can be particularly challenging for the Seven fixation. The desire to transcend fixation is likely to be made into a fun-filled "spiritual" adventure, which supports the ego structure of the Seven rather than uprooting it. Here, a Seven reports:

When I heard about this thing called "enlightenment" — Wow! That sounded good! And yet it had to have pizzazz. So, when I read a book by Osho about music and dance and sexuality, everything was okay! That really drew me to India and that's why I chose to live in the commune for seven years. The name he gave me was a Sufi word for one of the ninety-nine aspects of God, and its meaning is, "God is the destiny." So I thought, "Hey, I don't have to worry!"

The painful dilemma of the Seven's planning is that deciding on some specific thing or course of action is to die to all the other possibilities. Sevens find this intolerable. Being able to change plans and directions at a moment's notice gives them a feeling of being open to divine guidance.

Sevens feel they are part of the divine plan. In order not to mess up the plan, they must always keep their options open.

Sevens often talk about doing things for six months. Their passion of gluttony keeps them moving from relationship to relationship, job to job. Travel is a very important part of their world because it constantly brings new experience. Every Seven I know has traveled, often hitchhiking, usually inexpensively. Sevens were the first to discover the beaches of Goa in India, and were trekking in Nepal before it was fashionable. Many have made multiple pilgrimages to India and have gone swimming with wild dolphins.

One Seven I know planned a move to Boston from San Francisco. First, she went to Hawaii for a workshop; then she went to Bali. After returning to San Francisco, she made a short journey to New York, then to Boston. The process of moving to Boston took more than a year. Of course, once there, she was off traveling through Europe!

These are not necessarily wealthy people, although the classic Seven lives frugally off a small trust fund. I know a Chicano Seven who grew up in the barrio of east Los Angeles. He still doesn't have much money, but he manages to travel to Europe for half the year teaching Tai Chi workshops.

Childhood Setting

Sevens come from a full range of childhood situations. Initially, I expected them to come from well-to-do families, and many of them do. However, there are the examples like the one just mentioned. This is a man who was the fifth of seven children. He shared a bed with two brothers. His father was a furniture mover, and the boys had to help move furniture on the weekends. This Seven was the one who cracked jokes and kept things light; he cheered up the rest of the family. Now he does some standup comedy about growing up in the barrio, and travels around teaching workshops.

A female Seven described growing up in a poor black family, being chased by neighborhood bullies, and experiencing times without enough to eat. She made it sound like fun and enthralled her audiences with the story. She said she was having a great time back then, too.

One man reported that he had a miserable childhood filled with the tensions between his parents. His solution was to go out and play with his friends, making believe there was nothing wrong.

Sevens often report having trouble with their fathers and being closer to their mothers. They typically take an anti-macho position in life and embrace the feminine. A Seven's life is often a signal to Mom that everything is okay.

Idealization: "I am okay."

The idealization of the Seven is, *"I am okay."* Sevens are considered the most narcissistic of any of the Enneagram points. It is rare to find them in therapy, as it takes a sudden crisis to bring them to therapy. And then they usually don't stay long.

Many years ago, a Seven came to me because he knew I practiced NLP (Neuro-Linguistic Programming). His father was putting a lot of pressure on him to "grow up" and, in fact, was paying for the therapy. When asked what he really wanted, this Seven answered, "My cheap hustle isn't working anymore. I know the empire is falling and I just want to get by until it crashes. I would like you to use NLP to teach me to lie more effectively."

Sevens can be the hardest to reach because they have created an ego structure that to them appears to be an enlightened state. This is the meaning of "I am okay." Even deeper than "I am okay," the Seven response to any spiritual guidance is, "I know." These people are often conceptually enlightened, having heard it all and incorporated it into an air-tight belief structure. "Emptiness? Oh, yeah, I know, we're all one," is often the Seven response to the challenge of going deeper than the known.

Talking Style: Stories

The talking style of Seven is called *stories*. These are the con artists of the Enneagram. They can be charming, turning any event into a delightful story. The Broadway play, *The Music Man*, is the story of a Seven. The main character is a traveling salesman who comes to town to sell musical instruments. He does it by weaving a magical story that entrances everyone about the future town band. Kids save their nickels and pennies to buy the dream the Music Man is selling.

Timothy Leary, a Seven, went from being a Harvard college professor to a standup comic in nightclubs based on his ability to keep everyone laughing with his brilliant mind and charming stories. Many years ago now, there was an art show in San Francisco of blotter acid. Tim Leary was at the opening, where he announced that he had cancer and was putting his death live on the Internet as his last great trip.

Robin Williams was the classic Seven. His standup comedy is a tapestry of stories woven with brilliant improvisations. Perhaps the best example of his work in this style is the performance, *Live at Carnegie Hall*.

The Trap: Idealist

The trap of the Seven is called *idealist*. Idealism is part of the way the ego gets justified as enlightened. Sevens are true idealists: "Liberty, Equality, and Fraternity" is a Seven motto.

Sevens love to bring high and low together. One Seven I know was working as an aerobics teacher at a bank. She was ready to quit, but what kept her at her job was the delight of seeing the bank president and the janitor sweat together.

The Peace Corps is a Seven idea; Sergeant Shriver, one of its principle founders, was a Seven. Being a goodwill ambassador and helping the Third World comes from the Seven idealism.

This idealism often comes out when Sevens are under stress and move to the One position. It is very rare for a Seven to act out anger. Instead, in moving to One, they become sarcastic and moralistic about their idealism. They may start lecturing friends about eating organic food, or be quite sarcastic as a way of expressing anger in the justified position of their humanitarian ideals.

Defense Mechanism: Rationalization

The defense mechanism of the Seven is *rationalization*. Since everything is part of God's plan, anything can be rationalized.

"Go with the flow" is a Seven concept. (This has been updated in the spiritual community to, "Let go, and let God.") And yet the Seven is continually trying to manipulate the flow by planning. This is what makes their encapsulation so hard to crack. Everything is part of God's will and all is leading to a pleasant conclusion. So don't get upset . . . relax, and enjoy the ride.

Avoidance: Pain

Sevens avoid *pain*. In order to avoid pain, they keep relationships light and uncommitted. This keeps them skating on the surface of life. Another way they avoid pain is by staying in their heads with "magical thinking" about the future. Their fear of pain is a terrifying thing to them, much worse than the pain itself. However, most Sevens won't know this since they are generally very successful at avoiding pain in the first place.

To avoid pain, Sevens stay on the move, ever in pursuit of new experience. Avoidance of pain makes them charming conversationalists and sometimes brilliant thinkers. The lateral thinking of the Seven, and the new connections that are made, are attempts to enjoy the moment while avoiding the possible emotional depths of pain. The following story illustrates the avoidance of the Seven:

My friend who is a Seven never misses an opportunity to go to lunch. When she discovered her husband had cancer she agreed to go to lunch with a group of her friends, leaving her husband at home. There she humorously announced, "I married him for better or for worse — but not for lunch." She then discussed his disease and prognosis amid anecdotes and laughter laced with tears. She wasn't about to let his cancer and her friends' pain get in the way of having a light-hearted lunch.

In the following, a Seven shows how the pattern of avoidance works for him. Even in the telling of it, the speaker seems to play to the audience, keeping it light and getting some laughs:

I see how turning on the TV or doing 101 things can be ways not to have to be in the moment and feel the pain and terror. I just finished school, which had me going constantly. I was rarely bored. In these last three months since I've graduated, I've had a lot of time on my hands and it's been a bit uncomfortable. But I feel it is my responsibility to not be bored. That if I am bored, it's because I'm not using my resources to create excitement. That's what I want, and damn, I'm going to get it! So boredom be gone! (Laughter)

Dichotomy: Inferior/Superior

The dichotomy in Seven is called *inferior/superior*. When they meet a new group of people, they will sit quietly while evaluating the status and power relationships in the group. Once they understand where they fit in the hierarchy, they may move into action.

Some Sevens manifest the inferior side of this dichotomy, always putting themselves on the down side of any relationship. Inferior Sevens are often in quest of more information to help make decisions. They may be workshop fanatics in search of a strong leader. The inferior side may be subdued in public, allowing the magical thinking to manifest only in more intimate relationships.

The superior side of the dichotomy manifests as the con artist or charmer. Though I have yet to meet a Sexual Seven who manifested the inferior side of the dichotomy, I have known Self-preservation Sevens and Social Sevens on both sides.

Subtypes

Self-Preservation: Extended Family

When the passion of gluttony uses the Self-preservation instinct, it is called *extended family*. Self-preservation Sevens consider themselves part of an extended family. Communes are a manifestation of the Self-preservation Seven style. Not all Self-preservation Sevens live in communes, but they all consider their extended family closer than blood family.

I have a friend who is a Self-preservation Seven living in Budapest. He was one of the pioneers in bringing New Age culture to Hungary when it was still communist. Based on his extended family, he managed to travel around the world, including multiple trips to California and Hawaii, despite having only a little money (Hungarian money was useless outside of the country).

Social: Martyr

The Social Seven is called *martyr*. These people often appear to be perfect husbands and wives. They may live all their lives in one spot doing one job. This is because they are willing to martyr themselves and their fascination with new ideas, for the good of the family. Notice how this position is a variation of the duty of the Social Six; the sense of duty to the family creates the martyr in the Seven.

One Social Seven, a psychiatric nurse in San Francisco, has dreamed for years of taking his family backpacking through Europe. He has rationalized it in such a way that he wants his children to have the richness of experience that he has had. Although he has held this dream for years, he stays with the practicality of day-to-day life, making sure his children get a good education. He has martyred himself for the good of his family.

Another Social Seven, a successful workshop leader, came to me for therapy to become enlightened. He was afraid that this might mean giving up some of his pleasures, such as extra-marital affairs. He was almost ready to do that for his wife, whom he truly loved. But in the end, he didn't love her enough to martyr himself. They are now divorced.

Sexual: Suggestibility

The *suggestibility* of the Sexual Seven creates the condition of "monkey mind." Marked by a short attention span and continuous fascination with the new and exotic, the Sexual Sevens are the true "cosmic travelers."

It is extremely rare to find a Sexual Seven in a long-term relationship. The longest continuous relationship that I know of is two years. These are the hitchhiking gourmets, off to explore and enjoy the variety of the world's cultures.

Sometimes maligned as having the attention span of a chicken and the loyalty of a snake, Sexual Sevens can be loyal friends. They love to come into your life periodically and cheer you up or help you to deal with your problems. As long as you don't need them while they are off trekking in the Himalayas or sunning on the beach in Thailand, they can be long-term friends, loyal on their own terms. Just don't expect them to get too deeply into your pain, let alone theirs.

Additional Exemplars

I have a very dear friend, a Sexual Seven, who had been a history professor. After "dropping out" in his late twenties, he participated in the hippie spiritual scene, living in various spiritual communes. As he approached fifty, he thought he might like to settle down. He decided he was going to open a jewelry shop, either in Connecticut or San Francisco. He planned to stay with us for a few days every year on his annual pilgrimage from the East Coast to India and Nepal.

One year he checked out various sites for his shop before leaving for Asia. The next year, back from the East Coast and heading west, he told us that he had definitely narrowed his choice to one of three locations in Santa Barbara and San Francisco.

A year later, a store became vacant in the exact location he was considering. Faced with a moment of real choice, he realized that he didn't want to be tied down to being a shopkeeper after all. Several years later, he is still living comfortably on his investments and pondering what he is going to do when he grows up.

Cary Grant, also a Sexual Seven, grew up in a cockney slum in London. He changed his name, developed a new accent, and with his natural charm created a life of fame. Once, when asked the secret of success, he replied, "Always have a good suntan."

When asked the secret of his success with women, Porfirio Rubirosa, a Dominican playboy of the fifties, replied, "I have the fastest cigarette lighter in the house."

Ram Dass, a New Age guru, once said that while on the circuit he would "show up in town for a talk, smoke a joint, and go out and cheer them up."

Timothy Leary is perhaps the quintessential Seven. A former psychology professor, he left Harvard University for the spiritual potential of LSD. He became the guru of a generation with his famous motto encouraging everyone to try LSD: "Turn on. Tune in. Drop out!"

Leary once said in a Playboy interview that with LSD, men could experience multiple orgasms, having the best sex of their lives, while at the same time becoming conscious of their genetic code. Asked years later if he thought the statement was true, he said he made it up just for effect.

After being arrested for possession of marijuana, Leary was freed from prison by the Weatherman faction of Students for a Democratic Society. He was spirited to Algeria, where he spent time in exile with Eldridge Cleaver and the Black Panthers.

Leary, however, couldn't handle the down energy of revolutionary politics. Fleeing through Europe, he was again arrested in Afghanistan and brought back to the United States. He is perhaps the only person ever allowed to be the star of a film documentary while serving time in Folsom prison. He probably charmed the warden.

Having gone through several wives and dozens of lovers, Leary went from esteemed college professor to a stand-up comedian on the night-club circuit. His dozens of books are often brilliant, always entertaining, and filled with new ideas. Leary was the proponent of space migration and made a convincing argument that we are seeded by intergalactic intelligence. He once fabricated a message from the star Sirius and Intergalactic Command to further our belief in his message.

Calling him a con man is too coarse. He just had a touch of the blarney.

Exemplars by Subtype

Self-Preservation~Extended Family:

Andre Gregory, Danny Kaye, Roger Rabbit, Peter Pan, David Niven, Zonker Harris (Doonesbury), My Dinner with Andre, Swimming to Cambodia, Disney World

Social~Martyr:

George W. Bush, Jerry Seinfeld, Robin Williams, Spaulding Gray, Gary Hart, Steven Spielberg, Herb Caen, Michael Caine, Walt Disney

Sexual~Suggestibility:

Timothy Leary, Ram Dass, Bob Marley, Cary Grant, Bo Derek, Peter O'Toole, Brazil

Point Five: The Interiorized Fear Point

Essence:	Peace
Holy Idea:	Omniscience
Holy Path:	Nonattachment
Chief Feature:	Withdrawal
Passion:	Avarice
Idealization:	"I know"
Talking Style:	Treatise
Trap:	Observer
Defense Mechanism:	Isolation
Avoidance:	Emptiness
Dichotomy:	Social/Antisocial
Subtypes:	Self-Preservation~Home Social~Totem Sexual~Confidence

The interiorized version of Six, Fives unknowingly cover the essence of peace by trying to create peace through exclusion of the outside world. They deal with their fear by reducing life to manageable proportions. In the extreme, a Five might be a Buddhist monk living as a hermit in a cave with all his possessions in a little pouch.

Five is the home of architecture. Fives put a lot of thought into their living space. They enjoy small, tight, well-defined limits in their living area. They need to have their own living space. If they live with someone else, they need to have their own workroom, a place to get away. More than one Five has described having a travel trailer set up in the backyard. When company comes, they give up the house and retreat to the trailer, where there is just enough room for one.

Fives love to be the "house wizard." Always full of esoteric information on a vast variety of subjects, they enjoy holding court. Sharing secrets can be their indication of intimacy.

Fives are fiercely independent. While they don't act out like Eights, they are nonconforming rebels. Fives pride themselves on being able to take care of themselves. Many have had experiences of hitchhiking in foreign countries with very little money. Fives who haven't actually had this experience usually would like to. They find deep satisfaction in knowing they can survive on very little, and much pleasure being a stranger in a strange land.

The Five loves to be a "fly on the wall." At social gatherings they tend to disappear in the background. They sometimes seem like an owl on a perch, observing the rest of us with detached interest.

In appearance, Fives quite often have a very flat affect. They may seem invisible in a group of people. Beards, glasses, and sometimes weak chins are part of their disguise. They may also hide behind a nasal-sounding voice. They often have a repertoire of funny voices, speaking with a foreign accent or like a computer.

Fives are some of the most deeply sensitive people on the Enneagram. Their problem is they do not have much of a defense against the outside world. They retreat into a rich, phantasmagoric inner life, leaving an almost invisible apparition in the room with the rest of us.

Often, they have skin that is susceptible to sunburns and rashes. This becomes metaphoric for a tender sensitivity that needs protection from an abrasive world. One Five said this sensitivity was, "like walking through a cactus field with no skin."

Passion: Avarice

The passion in Five is *avarice*, which most dictionaries define as greed for money. Although Fives may be stingy with money, for most Fives the greediness is not for great wealth, but may in fact be quite the opposite: to hold on avariciously to the few things in the world they claim as their own. People who see the world through the lens of the Five usually require very little, for they are truly minimalists. They think that if they do not have much, then the world will leave them alone. Fives are also very greedy when it comes to their privacy; isolation becomes their way of defending against the intrusion of the world.

J. Paul Getty is a wonderful example of avarice in its most neurotic expression. He started his fortune by winning oil wells in a poker game. Although he was the wealthiest man in the world, he took his lunch to work in a brown paper bag. He had a pay phone installed in his castle in England so people wouldn't "mooch off him." He charged his children and guests twenty pounds each for lunch when they came to eat with him at the castle. When his grandson was kidnapped, he balked at paying the ransom — even after the kidnappers sent him his grandson's ear! His son had no money to pay the ransom, as the old man controlled it all. In the end he loaned his son the money, with interest, to pay the kidnappers.

He refused to go to bed for the last several months of his life because he said, "The bastards are just waiting for me to go to bed and die." Getty died in his chair.

Avarice often manifests in Fives as greed for information. The holy idea of the Five is omniscience. When taken into the ego structure, the Five believes that information will be the protection against the black hole of nothingness. Like Fours, Fives are very aware of this black hole that resides at the root of all ego. The fear of falling in, to never return, is countered by the belief that enough information will protect them from the black hole of extinction.

The avarice of Fives also manifests as a withholding of self. They are deathly afraid of losing themselves to the world. A Five once commented that if she opened herself to the world, someone would reach in, grab her heart, and tear it out. For the Five, it can seem as if they are perched between a black hole on the inside, and a threatening, invasive world on the outside. Avarice can be seen as the attempt to hold on to this narrow perch. Speaking in front of a group of workshop participants, a Five shared insight into how this works:

For me the black hole represents more than an idea. For me, it's like absolute obliteration and annihilation. Sometimes in the midst of it, there's no time to think. The feelings are too big. There's almost a cellular pulling in, like trying to protect myself. I can feel it right now in this situation. Although I know in my mind there's no danger here and that you're loving, there's a way in which your attention almost feels like an assault, like I am being attacked. So there is a fierceness, which is a survival imperative. It's like I can't allow you to push me with your ideas. I'm struggling so hard just to stay here altogether.

Walking on the beach today, the sun, the sand, and the sea were so overwhelming I just started crying. How can you be in the body when there's so much and let it all through? If it were plumbing, it would be like trying to fit a ten-inch pipe into a two-inch pipe. It's a primal frustration, and it's terrifying because in the fullness of everything there's just this constant feeling that I am going to explode into a thousand pieces and not be able to find myself amongst the pieces. That encourages this pulling in and hiding and immovability. This can be read like coldness, aloofness, or stubbornness. When I get read that way, it's deeply painful because underneath there's a deep longing to connect and be whole. It's just hard to do it through this body.

Fives can be great collectors. Unlike Nines, who accumulate stuff that will be useful someday, Fives collect and catalog rare and important items. I know a Five who was a struggling musician in New York. By chance he became interested in wine; within months he was a wine connoisseur and expert. He knew all the great vintages and the appropriate chateau for each vintage. He also knew where to find the best deals. He would call from New York to let me know about an excellent 1962 St. Estephe for only thirty dollars. Living frugally in a studio apartment, he has amassed a fifty-case wine collection in the space of five years.

Another Five collects records, which he has sorted and alphabetized. Tapes or compact discs would never do for him; the music is not as important as the vinyl recording. A Five in Mill Valley, California, ran one of the great record stores in the United States. An entire room is devoted solely to 78 RPM. He may have every great jazz and blues album ever recorded. He was there from the Sixties to the Nineties when rent raises drove him out. Other Fives have mentioned collecting shamanic flutes from the Amazon and sixteenth-century lutes.

John Barth, a brilliant American author, devotes a dozen pages in one of his later novels to describing his loose-leaf binder, bought as a freshman in 1947 and still in loving use. He also describes his beloved, sacred, Parker fountain pen bought in the same time period, which flows forth with the voice of the muse.

One Five described the passion of avarice on a more mundane level, that happened while driving along the border of Mexico on his way to a job in California. He was delighted to discover he could drive across the border and buy fifths of whiskey for a couple of dollars each. He would wait until evening so that when the border guard changed over, he could enter and return twice at each crossing, carrying the maximum allowed. Soon, he had so much whiskey he had to start shipping it ahead. A successful banker, now retired, he laughed and said that the whiskey lasted him for over twenty years. While I forgot to write it down when he told me, thirty years later, he still remembers the exact amount that he paid for the fifths.

Childhood Setting

Fives most always had an intrusive parent. Often it was an over-protective mother. They frequently report that their mother went through their drawers looking for clues about how "her baby" was doing. Fives often report a sense of being smothered by mother's love, or feeling suffocated by a lack of space.

One Five reported that when he was about seven years old, he had a fold-out of a Playboy bunny. He folded it into a tiny square, only inches across, hid this in a box, and hid the box in a secret place in his bedroom. When he returned from school, it was laid out on the bed awaiting his return.

With no place to hide, young Fives often retreat into their minds. One Five reported spending all her free time alone up in a tree. They retreat into books and scholarship as a way of creating free space.

Idealization: "I know."

The idealization of the Five is *"I know."* This feeds into their avarice for knowledge. But it can't just be knowledge that everyone else has; there has to be something special about it. Thus, Fives become investigative reporters, discovering "the story behind the story."

One Five, now in his thirties, still remembers the batting averages of his high school baseball team. He said the statistics were more important to him than who actually won the game.

Aldous Huxley not only knew all his work by heart, but under hypnosis could tell you which page a passage appeared on in different editions.

If Fives follow a spiritual path, they will know the guru's guru. I once set up a workshop for Claudio Naranjo, a Social Five, who is one of the experts on the Enneagram. He came in, sat on the floor, and built a semicircle of books around him. As he spoke, he would often look around, find a book, get engrossed in it, and forget about the workshop.

Talking Style: Treatise

The talking style of the Five is called *treatise*. A treatise is a written, systematic discussion of facts, methods, principles, and conclusions of a given subject. This is still another way of creating distance. Fives love the personal computer. They are often the computer hackers who spend long hours into the night, alone in front of a terminal. When they meet fellow computer nerds, they can spend hours talking technical intricacies as a way of avoiding intimacy. E-mail is an ideal communication medium for a Five; Fives refer to it as talking shop.

A friend once took his TV set in for repair. Out of the back room came a bearded, balding man with glasses. Peering back to his workspace, my friend noticed there was a special place for a coffee mug and a lever for bringing it over to the workspace. A great deal of time and thought had gone into that space. The man looked at my friend, smiling, and said, "Oh, yes, you probably burned out a Sylvania 232." There was a slight air of condescension toward anyone who didn't know what a Sylvania 232 was.

I notice in groups that the talking style of the Five is often silence. I have been in groups where a week has gone by, and just about everyone has shared something, except the Five, who is sitting quietly in the back. By the end of the week no one knows his name, and many are not yet aware that he is there. Often when Fives do speak in a group, there is a lack of volume, and everyone has to listen very intently just to hear what they are saying. In safe surroundings or friendly company, however, the Five can be funny and bright, as they explain the wonders of the world to you.

The Trap: Observer

The trap for the Five is being the *observer*. In this way, they stay disengaged from life. I know several Fives who practice Buddhist meditation. Taking the Buddha's dictum of nonattachment as their path, they believe they are unattached to the world. Yet, when confronted by this Enneagram system, they often admit to being attached to nonattachment.

True nonattachment is a byproduct of the realization of oneself as pure consciousness. In this realization, it is recognized that not only is nothing needed in this awareness, but there is also no need to avoid or withdraw from anything. One lives as the vast awareness in which all things arise, meeting each moment without attachment to preconceptions. Thus, the trap of observer can serve to trick the Five into perpetuating ego-structure in the name of enlightenment.

Defense Mechanism: Isolation

The defense mechanism of the Five is *isolation*. Obviously, this meshes very closely with the trap of observer. When Fives get into a fight, their style may be to leave the room and slam the door behind them. They often feel drained from too much contact with the world. Fives feel the need to retreat within their own borders to recharge themselves.

This can take the form of spending days at the library (a Five institution), months traveling in an area where they can't speak the language and no one knows them, or years as a hermit. One Five came to a month-long workshop at Esalen in a pickup truck with a camper on the back. He was quite happy to spend his time there living in the back of his truck. Another Five reported that he spent a lot of time on his computer in his home office, and that if the other adults in his household wanted to communicate with him, they had to pass notes under the door.

At the First International Enneagram Conference, two of the invited feature speakers were Fives. One didn't show up and the other sent a video tape.

Five is the place of suicides. The danger for Fives is getting so deeply lost in isolation that they lose all nurturing contact with the outside world. Here a Five speaks of the impulse to find safety and comfort through isolation:

I remember once when I was little, playing alone in a dark closet with imaginary toys and friends. It was probably the safest moment that I ever felt. But I knew that if I gave into that impulse, even though it was comfortable, I knew I wouldn't make it. So, I've been struggling against that impulse my whole life. I can't afford to give into the impulse to escape into an imaginary world, because if that happens, it's worse than this feeling of being so vulnerable.

Avoidance: Emptiness

The avoidance of *emptiness* may at first glance seem counter to the defense mechanism. Yet, the emptiness that Fives avoid is internal. The Five, like the Four, lives on the edge of the abyss. Sartre's black hole of nothingness is very real for them.

Feeling themselves living on the brink, Fives avoid the emptiness with an avarice for knowledge. They may sense that the black hole could be filled if only they knew enough. Or they may sense that knowledge — or anything else they happen to collect and cling to — acts as a protective barrier against the hurricane winds whipping through the black hole.

One Five, a brilliant German doctor doing leukemia research, told me he would never be enlightened because he would not give up his memories. This was so the Holocaust would always be remembered and never repeated. On his rare day off, he would take his reluctant girlfriend for a visit to Dachau.

He spent a week "hiding" in the group, and it was only after the group was over that he felt safe to speak to me. No one in the group knew he was doing blood research, looking for the cure for leukemia. He told me that most of his patients were children and that almost all of them would die. The tenderness and rawness with which he said this brought tears to his eyes and mine, as he described his search for the secret that would save lives.

The Dichotomy: Social/Antisocial

The dichotomy in Five is called *social/antisocial*. Which side of this dichotomy is manifested determines the Five's relationship with the world.

Social Fives, such as Henry Kissinger, can appear to be very public people. Howard Cosell, the TV sports announcer, was a Social Five. He made his living on having the inside scoop, the story behind the story. He befriended Muhammad Ali, and traded on what the boxer personally told him before a fight. His nasal voice is almost a caricature of the Five propensity for speaking from the back of the head through the nasal cavities.

Howard Hughes, the billionaire inventor, personified the antisocial Five. Hughes invented everything from seaplanes to a brassiere for Jane Russell. At the time one of the wealthiest men in the world, he lived for years as a phobic recluse. Terrified of germs, Hughes made people who entered his room touch everything with tissue as a means of avoiding spreading germs.

Subtypes

Self-Preservation: Home

When avarice is fueled by the Self-preservation instinct, it is called *home*. "A man's home is his castle" is surely a Five notion. This is the place of architecture. All Self-preservation Fives must have their own space. If they are not architects, they often dream of creating the perfect house. One man reported that his dream is to build a log cabin. He has spent twenty-six years researching how to build a log home by sketching his own designs, sending away for blueprints and catalogues, traveling to log home expositions, surfing the Internet for information, and combing his locale for the perfect lot.

Another Self-preservation Five, who is separated from his wife, lives in a camper. His two children come to visit him in his camper.

Though he loves the kids and loves to see them, he can't help feeling a sigh of relief when they finally stop invading his space.

The film *Mosquito Coast* is the story of a Self-preservation Five inventor who takes his family to live in the jungle, away from hated society.

Social: Totem

When avarice uses the social instinct, it is called *totem*. Totem means the ritual power of an object beyond its normal functionality. This is the power books have over book collectors, and records have over record collectors. For John Barth, it is his fountain pen. For the Social Five, this power is often bestowed on information, especially on having the story behind the story. This is the natural home of investigative reporters. Fives always have secrets. Sharing a secret with you is their way of being intimate.

Sexual: Confidence

Sexual Fives display *confidence* in their sexuality. They know they are lovable, perhaps because they were truly loved as children. They also have confidence in playing a role, which they in fact play most of the time, even in private. Behind the role-playing they hide their feelings of uncertainty, vulnerability, and shyness, as well as their terror of invasive demands and exposure. Some of the finest actors are Sexual Fives: Meryl Streep, Glenn Close, William Hurt, Jeremy Irons, Jeff Bridges, and Ben Kingsley.

Additional Exemplars

Barak Obama is a Sexual Five. Smart, funny and a good man, he lacked the fiery anger that may have been needed to push through his agenda. His efforts at conciliation did not succeed and his compromises weakened his agenda. One wished he had his Sexual Eight's father's balls.

Classical China was a Five culture in which scholarship was worshipped. China had the first true civil service based on merit. To enter the civil service was the highest good to which one could aspire. Passing the exams required the ability to compose poetry, and having skill in painting and calligraphy. After a career in the government, the scholar/official retired to his country home to live simply — often a hermit existence — and practice his poetry, painting, and penmanship.

The Chinese are the great art collectors of the world. They have been amassing family art collections for at least 2,000 years. And what do they collect? Penmanship! Calligraphy by the great painters is one of the most esoteric and revered items for collection. Since most Chinese cannot even read this old-fashioned historic/ancient writing, being able to judge the merits of this penmanship is an extremely rare talent indeed. The Chinese see the character of the man expressed in his penmanship and collect examples from the great painters of the past centuries as a way of collecting essence.

Chinese painting also exemplifies the Five aesthetic. The finest and best is dry ink brush painting — black ink on rice paper. The best examples use the fewest minimalist strokes to create an inner feeling of the landscape perceived by the artist. The dry barrenness of this art form is appreciated by only a very few.

San Francisco had an animation festival to honor several film animators, all of whom must have been Fives. It was painful to watch them standing on stage, trying to be invisible. They edged to the back of the stage and found it impossible to answer any of the questions put to them by the moderator. One person actually made a mistake introducing himself, giving a wrong name. These people spend years alone with storyboards. They spend years at home in their studio, working on a project that they know from the outset will end up as a five-minute, noncommercial art piece.

One of the awards was for an animated pin board. The result of three and a half years of staying home, photographing the shadows and textures created by moving pins in and out on a board, was a ten-minute short subject that no one would ever see except at an occasional animation festival. But it was a good excuse to stay in one's room.

J. D. Salinger, the novelist famous for *Catcher in the Rye*, sued a would-be biographer to protect his privacy and block publication of the book. Salinger, who has an extremely small number of books in print for a writer of his prominence, allowed that he continued to write, but only for himself. He had not been photographed in public, nor had he given an interview in over forty years. He gave his last newspaper interview in 1953. A student who lived in a community near Salinger's home reported the following story:

J.D. Salinger would come into the local shoe store once a year and order new shoes. He would order two pairs, which he would then pick up when they were ready. This went on for several years. Most people in the community did not realize Salinger was famous and didn't really take much notice of him. The shoe store owner was no exception. One year the storeowner was made aware that Salinger was a well-respected writer and decided to read his work. Upon Salinger's next yearly visit to the store, the owner let him know that he really enjoyed reading one of his books. Salinger walked out, never returned to the store, and didn't even pick up the shoes he had ordered.

Karl Marx was writing his revolutionary pamphlets and books at a time when Europe was rocked by revolution. Instead of joining the Paris Commune (as an Eight would have done), or any of the other revolutions that broke out across Europe, Marx stayed in England, doing his daily writing at the London library.

On the other hand, W.C. Fields was a comic genius. His brilliance as a comic artist lives on after him, and his voice is still distinctive years after his death. He started in show business as a pantomiming juggler. Once in films, he took the position of being an outsider in a strange land and made it into a comic art form. Fiercely independent, Fields' dislike of noisy children, birds, pets, and intrusive, bossy wives was a staple of his comedy.

Exemplars by Subtype

Self-Preservation~Home:

J. Paul Getty, Dick Cheney, Dustin Hoffman, Gene Wilder, Ted Kaczynski was both a social critique and The Mail Bomber, Thomas Merton, Albert Camus, J.D. Salinger, R. Crumb, W.C. Fields, Franz Kafka, Aldous Huxley, Lao Tzu, architecture, hermits

Social~Totem:

Thomas Jefferson, Henry Kissinger, Ruth Bader Ginsberg, Jonas Salk, Kurt Vonnegut, Mark Twain, Karl Marx, Bob Dylan, Harry Potter, John Barth, Lenny Bruce, Albert Einstein, Walter Cronkite, rare book collectors, inventors, investigative reporters, Data (Star Trek)

Sexual~Confidence:

Meryl Streep, Glenn Close, Barack Obama, Elijah Wood, William Hurt, Ben Kingsley, Jake Gyllenhaal, Jeremy Irons, Ingmar Bergman, Gary Snyder, Marlene Dietrich, Spencer Tracy, Jimmy Stewart, Howard Hughes

Movement and Relationships of the Points

Secondary Teachings

There are many different relationships between each of the fixations. As you study and absorb this system, you will find relationships between the fixation and its bordering points. An Eight
will have qualities of both Nine and Seven. Eights can have the
gluttony of the Seven and the indolence of the Nine. Don Riso and
Russ Hudson have contributed the study of "wings" to describe the
different personalities as a fixation leans to one side or the other.
While this study is quite accurate, the deeper issues that underlie
the personality are more interesting.

Each fixation is also in a relationship with two others, by
connected lines of the Enneagram. Some theorize that it is better
to move in one direction and destructive to move in another. In
truth, there are lessons to be learned at each of the points.

This movement happens either in a relaxed state or a state of
stress. The shift in the relaxed direction is sometimes called the
"heart space." Calling this a "heart space" can be misleading because in the realization of the true heart, there is a transcendence
of fixation altogether. Within the context of being fixated, however, calling this movement "dropping deeper into the core" may be
more descriptive and useful.

Fixations are nested. The primary fixation is wrapped around a
deeper one at the core, and there is a more superficial one above.
This is useful to know for two reasons. First, it can help with diagnostics. More importantly, it shows the underlying, unexamined
patterns that need to be faced.

Three, Six, and Nine: Movement of the Core Points

Three, Six, and Nine form the core points of the Enneagram. These points are connected by the inner triangle. On this triangle, the movement into the "core" is clockwise. In stress, the movement is counter-clockwise.

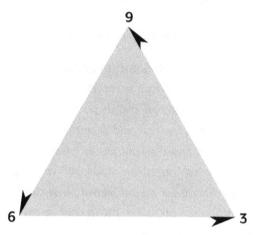

Three, Six, and Nine: Movement in Stress

Point Three

A Three in stress acts like a Nine. Instead of being productive, Threes will fantasize about production, moving out of action and into thoughts. A Three woman we know was raised as a working-class Mexican American. All her childhood training had taught her that women were not supposed to be successful in the world. Yet, living divorced in California in the 1980s, she wanted very badly to be successful at her career. The conflict created stress and a situation of fantasizing about her work, instead of working.

The character Willie Loman in *Death of a Salesman* is a vivid picture of a Three in stress. What is being avoided is the Nine's fear of loss of control. If this fearful rage is invited and experienced, then the bliss of true love can be realized.

Point Six

A Six in stress acts like a Three and starts producing. Many Sixes think they should be Threes and try to produce like Threes. Unfortunately, this is a stress space and leads to exhaustion and burnout. The value of this movement for Sixes is that it gets them out of their head and into production. The opportunity is to experience the terror and the worthlessness that drives it all. Underneath is true love.

Point Nine

A Nine in stress will act like a Six, getting caught in the loop of self-doubt and paranoia. Nines will not be sure of what is real, or if things are really the way they appear to be. In this state, decisions will swirl through their heads, with endless dialogues with themselves. The opportunity is for the Nine to experience the fear, which is under the doubt, and to drop more deeply into true emptiness.

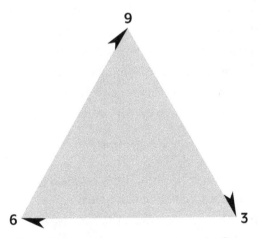

Three, Six, and Nine: Dropping into the Core

Point Three

When Threes fall in love, they drop into the core, which is the Six. This means that love and emotion are avoided by becoming more mental. They withdraw and start taking inventory, making lists of the beloved's qualities.

They start to assess how those they are trying to impress will view the relationship. They start trying to see behind the scenes to discover what is really going on. Thus, the feeling of love is avoided through mental processes.

Doubt seems overwhelming. In engaging in internal arguments with the doubt, the mental process continues. The opportunity is to use the doubt of the Six as a signal that fear is being avoided — in this case, the fear of losing control to the feelings of love. When the doubt becomes a signal of the fear of love, rather than an adversary in the mind, the fixation itself is the vehicle to approach what is being avoided.

Point Six

Six drops into Nine in the core. The Six relaxes, and paranoia melts into laziness. When they finally let their guard down and relax, some Sixes talk of spacing out in front of the TV or just collapsing onto a beach and not moving for a week. What is being avoided is true being. Once fear is gone, doing something switches to doing nothing, or laziness as an imitation of being. The opportunity is to feel the Nine's tendency to fall asleep to avoid rage and despair and remain awake, alert, and not-moving in the face of everything.

Point Nine

A Nine in the core will fall into Three, producing for the beloved. The Nine may make elaborate gifts, buy gifts, or take on new responsibilities. In some way, the Nine will start generating productive energy for the beloved. This is the way to avoid true love in the activity that is supposed to signal true love. This is the Nine's opportunity to experience the worthlessness and self-hatred of the Three, as well as the need to produce a lovable product. In the willingness to experience the deep self-hatred, true love reveals itself.

One, Two, Four, Five, Seven, and Eight: Movement of the Adjacent Points

The Enneagram is a mathematical system that has an infinitely repeating series. If you take the number 1 and divide it by 7, the result gives you an infinitely repeating sequence that starts with .1428571. This is the movement in stress for the numbers adjacent to the inner triangle. To find the movement into the core, just reverse this sequence.

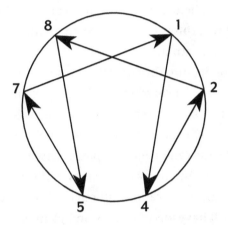

Movement in Stress for Points 1, 4, 2, 8, 5, 7

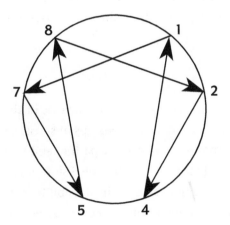

Movement into Core for Points 1, 4, 2, 8, 5, 7

We will now follow the numbers in the above order and notice what happens when each point moves into stress or drops into the core.

Point One

A One in stress starts to adopt some of the strategies of the Four, becoming melancholy and moody. Ones may long for the good old days as the past takes on a hazy, warm glow of perfection. They may look around and be envious of other people whose lives seem to be working out better. What is being avoided is the self-hatred of the Four. When this is faced and experienced, true golden joy is discovered underneath it.

A One dropping into the core takes on some of the characteristics of a Seven. A relaxed One may enjoy planning trips and looking at maps. Ones also enjoy labor-saving gadgets that seem to be a blend of the One practicality and Seven playfulness. The Swiss army knife, electric can-openers, apple peelers, and dishwashers are most likely inventions by Ones. Ones in the core may travel and may even enjoy a vacation, although it is more than likely that the trip will have lots of activity and planned excursions. What is being avoided is the Seven's terror of not knowing. When there is a willingness to surrender all knowing, all concepts, and all powers of conceptualization, the mind drops into the limitless bliss of being.

Point Four

A Four in stress will act like a Two, taking care of the power figure. Sometimes Fours start new relationships in stress, and at first, they act like Twos. They will defer to the partner and take care of the partner. They will move out of their own suffering, put on a cheery face, and be the helpful partner. The possibility is to drop through the pride and self-hatred of the Two to the essence of kindness.

A Four dropping into the core acts like a One. When Fours feel relaxed, open, and off-guard, they will tend to become angry perfectionists, noticing the flaws and subtle imperfections of the mate.

This movement plays into the Four's eternal melodrama of abandonment and lack of self-worth. When a man first comes into the Four's life, he is the perfect Prince Charming. She may be in stress and may treat him like a king. Once she gets to know him and settles in deeper, she may get bitchy and hypercritical. In this way, she drives away yet another love and her life becomes a self-fulfilling prophecy.

The possibility for the Four in the core is to feel the angry, internalized self-hatred of the One without moving. Falling in beyond this reveals the purity of essential perfection. When a Four has dropped beyond the fixation, this purity shines forth as a clear light to guide others home.

Point Two

A Two in stress acts like an Eight. The Two can rage and throw things in a wild temper tantrum.

An executive secretary I know, a Self-preservation Two, works for an accountant. One day she went to make a large cash deposit at the bank, but the bank was already closed when she arrived. She started pounding on the door and demanding to be let in. "It's ME!" she proclaimed. She was demanding that they recognize her pride of place. When the bank didn't open just for her, she became furious. The next day, filled with vengeance, she called every client in her office that had an account in that bank and had them close their accounts. The bank was forced to leave the location in this small town within the year.

The possibility for the Two in stress is to feel the raging vengeance of the Eight without moving. Under it is lust for power, and under the lust for power is the source of power. This is the experience of the shakti, the power of creation.

In the core of the Two lives a romantic Four. Twos often give up chasing romance, in their quest to be the perfect mother or mate. But the romance is always there, just below the surface. Twos love romance and the excitement of fresh love. In the addiction to the Four's hormonal rush of emotion, the Two is avoiding self-hatred. When self-hatred is faced and passed through, true joy is waiting.

Point Eight

An Eight in stress withdraws into Five. Some Eights I know speak of certain years, such as in high school, when they were under constant stress. At those times they retreated into their rooms, became anti-social, and read books. The Five space is the opportunity for the Eight to go deeply inward. The movement into Five can also be a way of avoiding painful truth. One Eight, when pressured by his wife to change his habits, would withdraw into a magazine as a way of avoiding seeing what was really present. The opportunity for the Eight in stress is to feel the fear and the isolation of the Five and, in surrendering the avarice of knowing, to discover the true peace below the surface.

One could say that nested in the core of the Eight outlaw is a Two mother. However, when an Eight starts taking care of someone, it is done as an Eight, meaning it is overdone. For dinner, the Eight will make too many different hors d'oeuvres and have too many bottles of wine. Everything is done from the Eight perspective that more is better, which is all running on unexamined pride. When the pride of the Two is faced, then the deep unlovability can also surface. Under this unlovability is found the true kindness that needs no recognition or reward.

Let me give you a personal example. As a Sexual Eight fixation when I fall in love I have discovered that I become, what I can only call, a bimbo! I stop thinking clearly and suddenly my universe revolves around my beloved. I don't have any needs, except to take care of her. I become, as the *Oklahoma* musical says, "A Girl Who Can't Say No."

Point Five

When Fives are in stress, they move towards Seven. The Five starts planning for the future and may begin traveling. This is a way to avoid the Seven's terror of not knowing, and the emotional pain under that. The possibility is to surrender all knowing, and plunge within to the deep, blissful absorption that is waiting below the surface.

Nested in the core of a Five is an outlaw Eight. Fives are the least conformist of any point on the Enneagram. When relaxed and dropped into the core, they may boast, become grandiose, or shout and then slam doors. However, they almost never will act out anti-social behavior like the Eight. When a Five acts out anti-socially, it is more like Ted Kaczynski mailing letter bombs through the postal service to avoid immediate contact. Meyer Lansky, the brains behind the Mafia, was a Five, but was never involved in actual violence.

Fives will hold anti-social opinions and side with the underdog. Once they have given their loyalty or made up their mind, they can become immovable in their determination. The great opportunity for the Five in the core is to feel the lust of the Eight without moving. Dropping through the lust brings the shakti of true being, and the true nourishment that is sought.

Point Seven

Sevens in stress become angry and judgmental like Ones. They may seem to be opinionated and cranky, as they lose the charming veneer of the Seven. What is being covered is the One's rage at imperfection, which is unbearable to feel internally, so it is projected out onto the environment. The possibility is to drop into the fear of not knowing and surrender the mind into the purity of perfection.

In the core of a Seven is a Five. Sevens have the Five's love of living cheaply and holding on tightly to the money they have.

The Seven's dance away from commitment and intimacy is another version of the Five's withdrawing from intimate contact. The Seven, having a Five heart, generally feels too vulnerable and delicate to let anyone get too close. Love of the adventure of being a stranger in a strange land is common both to the Five and the Seven, as this is a way to be simultaneously incognito and safely in touch with people. Acting, performing, and music can serve the same function. The opportunity for the Seven in the core is to drop all clinging to ideas and sensory experience, and fall into the deep peace of silence.

PART III

WAKING UP:
ESSENCE, TRANSCENDENCE,
AND SILENCE

How shall I speak of the Whole, which is non-dual? How shall I speak of the Whole, which is of the nature of duality? How shall I speak of the Whole, which is eternal and non-eternal? I am the nectar of Knowledge, homogeneous Existence, like the sky.

– Avadhuta Gita

To move from an identification as a limited fixation to the true identification as "Homogeneous Existence" has been the most rare of all events. The few who have awakened to their true identities have been celebrated through the ages.

Marrying Two Traditions

While I always assumed that self-inquiry arose in India, I have since learned that the investigation or inquiry into the self started 2,500 years ago in the Hellenistic culture of the Mediterranean. Why it arose here and flourished in Athens is a question I have been pondering for some time.

For one, the Ionian islands off the coast of what is now Turkey were at the borderline of Europe and Asia where they were influenced by several cultural streams. They were touched by the Phoenician trading culture that spread from Tyre in present day Lebanon to the founding of a colony in Carthage in North Africa. They were also in direct contact with the Persian and Babylonian cultures and they considered the Egyptians as their elder brothers. All this fed into a more cosmopolitan world view.

I believe it was the alphabet that first came from Phoenicia that was the tipping point. The Hebrews, as captives in Babylon, received the Hebrew alphabet, as a derivation of the Aramaic alphabet, Aramaic being the trading language of the Babylonians and Phoenicians. Both the Hebrews and the Greeks started their literacy by writing down the oral tradition. The near stone-age battle of Troy carried for generations as a poetic song/chant was written down as the Iliad and the Odyssey. We would now call it a myth. The Hebrews wrote the Five Books of Moses, known as the old testament, as a recording of the ancient oral lineage traditions and a mix of the stories they picked up while in captivity in Babylon, where the book was written. We could say it was the first of the genre called historical fiction.

Once reading replaces hearing as the seat of learning in the brain, the phonetic "alpha-bet" (alpha for Greek, Bet for Hebrew) that forces us to see the sounds that make up a word instead of the older scripts that use symbols, re-orders our thinking into a linear process. The Hebrews, after the founding document of the bible, were then concerned with the Talmud and commentaries, which I believe represent the linearization of their thinking about religion.

For the Greeks, or Ionians, this linear thinking took a different bent and turned towards examining what is real, what is it to be a human, and how to live a good life of happiness.

This book is an attempt to show how to integrate the Enneagram from the Greek philosopher Pythagoras with the transmission of silence from Ramana Maharshi, (which is equivalent to sudden awakening in the Zen tradition). Together they open a direct path to liberation.

Now it is possible for everyone to wake up. You do not have to be born a yogi or a saint. The teaching of my teacher Papaji is that the only requirement is the willingness to put aside everything you believe to be real, in order to discover the truth of reality. Without this total willingness, success will remain elusive regardless of practices or techniques. When willingness to see the truth is present, the whole universe supports your awakening. Then the Enneagram can be very powerful medicine to cure the illusionary ills of a fixated mind.

Since unlimited conscious love is ultimately discovered to be who you already are, any search for yourself is a movement in the wrong direction. The more you search, the further away you move from the truth of reality. When you are willing to uncover what is already here, you discover everything.

The quickest escape from the idea of a limited personal entity is to not move. Non-movement does not mean being physically still, although at the beginning stages physical stillness can be a great support. Rather, movement and non-movement relate to the mental and emotional bodies. To "move" is to follow mental and emotional thought waves in reactive patterns of fixation.

The secret meaning of non-dual wisdom is primordial enlightenment beyond action and effort.

— Vajrasattva to his devotee Vajrapanni

The Holy Idea

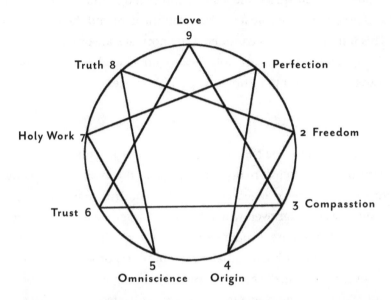

Love
9

Truth 8

1 Perfection

Holy Work 7

2 Freedom

Trust 6

3 Compasstion

5
Omniscience

4
Origin

In truth, no idea is holy and there is no path. What is holy is beyond any idea, and no path can ever reach the truth of oneself.

What, then, is the use of the holy idea in the Enneagram? The possibility is for the holy idea to be the galvanizing force behind the desire to transcend oneself and to die to every idea of a separate egoic entity. It allows the egoic mind to focus all its attention toward the discovery of what is beyond the mind. The holy idea is an ego-transcending idea. It captures the attention of egoic consciousness and points to the annihilation of ego. When the entire being — including mind, body, and emotions — yearns for freedom, then the value of the holy idea can be realized.

Each fixation mostly uses the holy idea as further justification for fixation. The holy idea becomes captured by the superego.

The simplest way to understand the super-ego is to realize that egoic mind lives in duality. The primal duality of man and God is internalized into the idea of a doer and the judge of the doer. The fixated idea of oneself is as a human doer, and God is internalized as the super-ego judge. This dialogue keeps the egoic structure in place. The function of the super-ego is to set limits, generate feelings of inadequacy and shame, and to judge and blame oneself and others. This sets up a war between the doer and the judge. This warfare is what is considered the normal state of life.

The super-ego uses the holy idea to judge the doer and the doer uses the holy idea to justify acting out its desires.

• • •

The holy idea for the Nine fixation is *love*. In the name of love, the Nine fixation will justify not staying true in the moment, if staying true might produce anger. The super-egoic judgmental fear of rage suppresses the rage even when it is the appropriate response. Once the natural response is suppressed, then the manifesting behavior is one of fixation. It is a habitual, mechanical response in the name of love. In the Nine's case, that usually means going to sleep, or not taking a stand when circumstances get heated or dangerous. Thus, the Nine will often not speak up for what is obviously right, and will then feel angry and resentful toward the other. The Nine becomes the helpless victim filled with blame and self-hatred. The Nine's "story" of love means not expressing what you feel, or even feeling what you feel. One should feel love; if one feels angry instead, well, that isn't loving, so it's better to go numb and space out.

In the actual experience of oneself as love, there are no rules about how love acts. Love is spontaneous and free, without condition. Love naturally loves love. Love supports love, and love reflects love. What this means and what form or behavior this takes is beyond the fixated mind's ability to grasp.

• • •

The holy idea for the Eight fixation is *truth*. The Eight uses the idea of truth as a club to beat everyone into submission, thereby maintaining dominance and control. When truth is used as a weapon, there is always an underlying idea of "my truth." Making truth subjective and personal is a lie.

In the realization of eternal truth, there is no separate one who exists to take anything personally. Truth is beyond all ideas and can inform every idea. Truth is formless and manifests as all form. Truth is the knowledge of oneself as the source of all of manifestation.

• • •

For the One fixation, the holy idea is *perfection*. When the superego of the One fixation incorporates the *idea* of holy perfection, it becomes reinforcement for the tendency to judge what is imperfect. Since perfection is an idea in the mind, it must always be viewed in polarity to some idea of imperfection. Imperfection must be found and noted to support the holy idea of perfection.

True perfection is not an idea at all; it is simply seeing things as they are. In true perfection, everything is included. Since nothing is separate from perfection, where can there be imperfection?

• • •

The holy idea for the Three is *compassion*. When the Three fixation owns the idea of compassion, it becomes a thought about doing the right thing. Any doing that is justified by the thought of compassion is ultimately a self-betrayal, because it is a contrived imitation of compassion arising from the moral code of a doer. All actions arising out of an imitation of true compassion eventually lead to suffering; someone will be left feeling unappreciated or unfulfilled.

True compassion is the spontaneous overflowing of an open heart. When the heart is broken all the way open, love pours out to benefit all beings. This is the way of the compassion of the bodhisattva and is transcendent of any particular fixation. True compassion has no giver, no receiver, and no act of giving. It is the spontaneous arising of love.

· · ·

Freedom is the holy idea of the Two. When the Two fixation uses freedom as a holy idea, it justifies prostituting itself as an act of free will. The Two's idea of freedom is to escape from the bondage of servitude to a desert island where there is no one to take care of. The implication is that the fixation is never free from the obligation to take care of others. The Two's obsessive need to care for others is a way of avoiding seeing that caring for others is, in fact, a selfish desire to extract love for oneself.

True freedom is not owned by any fixation. The desire for true freedom leads to the liberation of the soul, and the end of the Enneagram of Character Fixation. Freedom is the only real choice in a lifetime. All choices made from fixation are mechanical, predictable, having neither weight nor free will. The choice to be free is the only true, and final choice that arises in a lifestream.

Once freedom is chosen, the fixated life is surrendered. This surrender is the giving up of following choices driven by fixation. Then life is without choice. When freedom is in control, there is no one choosing and nothing to choose. Personal control has been surrendered, so that personal choice has no real meaning. Life then flows without choice as a divine expression of love.

True desire for freedom is the last desire of the ego. Before this desire arises, the fixated ego is lost in myriad desires and fears. Spiritual maturity is the willingness to put all desires into one final desire for freedom. This final desire leads the egoic mind to its surrender in the face of something huge and unknown. When the ego is willing to die for freedom, it will eventually face its death and die. What remains is what is untouched by death, and the deathless soul realizes itself as immortal consciousness. This is the end of the search and the beginning of true love.

• • •

Origin is the holy idea of point Four. When the Four fixation uses the idea of origin, it is seen as existing someplace else: "Wherever I find myself, the source must be somewhere else." It is through this belief that the fixation justifies its endless emotional search for fulfillment.

True origin is everyone's Buddha nature. It is the true, empty intelligence that is the ground of being. When you know yourself as the source of everything, you are Self-realized. There is no thought, no form, and no movement separate from source. Any thought, any form, or any movement arises from the field of emptiness, is made of emptiness, and returns to emptiness. Realizing this, the realized one has no problem with thoughts, forms, movements, or their absence.

• • •

The holy idea for the Six fixation is *trust*. When trust is incorporated into the mind's defenses as a holy idea, it exemplifies enslavement by fanatical religion. All cults are fear-based and driven by the super-ego's idea of trust. Trust, then, becomes blind trust. The possibility of betraying one's basic, inherent goodness arises from relying on a system of thought and morality to make decisions. All fundamentalist religious movements use trust as a weapon of the mind to beat down the spontaneous expression of the unknown. Blind trust removes one from the basic, intelligent wisdom of the heart and implants a super-ego parading as God to determine all action.

Trusting oneself is a different matter. Fixation is the lack of self-trust. In truth, trust may be needed at the very edge of the abyss before the jump into the unknown. Trust can be the antidote to fear. Fear is the contraction from jumping; but with trust in yourself, you can be afraid and jump anyway.

• • •

For the Seven fixation the holy idea is *holy work*. Any "idea" of holy work justifies the continued acting out of the fixation's desires in the name of holy work. Once the idea is incorporated into the super-ego, there can be guilt about not doing what is conceptualized as holy work, and then an endless search for the proper holy work.

True holy work never leads to realization because it is itself a by-product of realization. When the ego finally surrenders to the unknown love that dwells consciously in the heart, when one's life becomes truly dedicated in service to love, then the life itself is holy work.

Ramana Maharshi, for example, never left his beloved mountain. He never preached, and he never sought to convert or influence anyone. By simply being himself, he helped those who came asking for help. His incarnation was itself the holy work that touched untold numbers by its transmission of silence.

• • •

The Five fixation's holy idea is *omniscience*. When taken into the ego structure, the idea of omniscience becomes a goal in the future, that can be fulfilled by learning everything important. In this way, the mind justifies attachment to its precious mental objects. This attachment to thought is the obstacle to true omniscience.

True omniscience is the state of an empty mind. By not knowing anything in particular, consciousness is available to know whatever presents itself. This intelligent not-knowing is sometimes imitated by the thought of not knowing, as in, "I don't know." But this is usually a declaration of ignorance, not true liberation. True not-knowing is blissfully empty and clear.

• • •

The Holy Path

The Way does not require cultivation — just don't pollute it. What is pollution? As long as you have a fluctuating mind, fabricating artificialities and contrivances, all of this is pollution. If you want to realize the Way directly, the natural Mind is the Way. What I mean by the natural Mind is the mind without artificiality, without subjective judgments, without grasping or rejection.

– Chan Master Mazu China 12th Century

The Enneagram is a description of the fluctuating mind. The holy path is really not a path at all. It is the willingness to not move in the face of the impulse of fixation. Acting out fixation is the pollution, the artificialities that appear as the content of mind.

No path can take you to your true Self because you already are your true Self. Any path implies someone going somewhere else in search of something. This is called ignorance or samsara.

When you realize that what you are searching for is that which is conducting the search, you can stop all searching, all paths, and discover what is already and always present. What is ever-present is the ground of eternal being.

Tibetan Buddhism refers to this pristine ground of pure being as the Truth Body, or *dharmakaya*, another name for the Absolute. Your true body is empty, intelligent awareness that is the ground of the universe. The soul, or *sambhogakaya*, which the Tibetans translate as the Utility Vehicle of Pleasure, incarnates lifetime after lifetime in search of the path home to God.

Wherever you are in this moment is the end of the path if you are willing to bear the stopping of egoic identification. For each fixation, this stopping takes on different qualities.

. . .

Point Nine

For point Nine, the holy path is called *right action*. When the Nine is willing to stop indulging in fixation, everything that was previously avoided will appear. Since the pattern of the Nine is to avoid conflict at any cost, conflict will appear. Going numb, spacing out, agreeing with what is being said, and pretending not to have a preference are all the ways that the Nine avoids conflict. The Nine then feels victimized by not taking a stand and resents the other for being in control.

In the willingness to not move back into fixation, right action for the Nine is to stand in integrity in the moment, even if it's uncomfortable. In the willingness to face what has been avoided, the homicidal rage that runs the fixation will emerge from the murky depths to be experienced and burned.

. . .

Point Eight

Innocence is the holy path for point Eight. The Eight fixation takes the idea of innocence and uses it to blame others and proclaim oneself blame-free. The path of innocence then becomes a conceptual weapon of the ego to keep the Eight fixation firmly in control. The Eight fixation is a frightened child in a suit of armor. When the armor of competence and the certainty of being right are removed, the innocent child can emerge naked and without weapons.

True innocence cannot be practiced; it is a byproduct of true surrender. What the Eight fixation *can* do is give up being *right*.

The Eight can always assume that any critical feedback is correct. This creates the friction and the heat to burn the arrogance of believing oneself to always be right. When being right is truly surrendered and the distinction of right and wrong falls away, then true innocence shines as a confirming sign.

This is the preparation of the ground for realization. Until the Eight fixation can approach naked and innocent, the gateway of immaculate purity remains closed. Upon passing through the gate, the bliss of self-realization is the fruit.

• • •

Point One

The holy path for the One is called *serenity*. The tendency for the One is to have a glimpse of true reality and then to immediately conceptualize it into an idea of what that means. For the One to stop indulging in fixation, he must give up being right by surrendering all concepts. This brings up enormous fear, which is the barrier to be passed through. Stopping the habit of mentally grasping in order to be right exposes the terror of being wrong. In experiencing this terror without moving, serenity reveals itself. From here, the true investigation begins.

• • •

Point Three

For point Three the holy path is called *veracity*. Veracity is the willingness to bust the essential lie and self-betrayal of the fixation. Every Three is terrified of love and avoiding a deep self-hatred. This terror is covered with an act of being lovable, and the whole game is a lie. Since the fixation is based on a deep self-hypnosis that it is being truthful all the time, Threes believe they are being honest when they say that none of those feelings are even there.

Veracity requires exposing the lie, and experiencing the isolation, pain, fear, despair, and self-loathing that have been avoided so completely.

. . .

Point Two

For the Two fixation the holy path is *humility*. The Two runs on pride; humiliation is the antidote to pride. While no one relishes humiliation, it has the potential to be a great cleansing. It is like an acid that eats away at the encrusted layers of pride.

The great trap of humility is that, practiced as an idea or concept, it reinforces spiritual pride. True humility is often revealed as a result of the deep humiliation of being found out. One cannot practice humility, but one can welcome the calamity of humiliation. Welcoming humiliation does not mean creating it, but rather being open to whatever appears without resistance.

. . .

Point Four

The holy path for point Four is called *equanimity*. Equanimity is a balance in the emotional body. Yet, one cannot practice equanimity. Any practice will suppress the unexperienced emotions of the deeper layers. Since the Four fixation is addicted to emotional highs and lows, equanimity is thought of as a deadness. There is a great fear of equanimity among the more emotionally immature of the Four fixation.

The only way to true equanimity is to first be willing to give up the story of suffering. Without this willingness, nothing will be successful. With this willingness it is possible to experience everything that has been avoided, without taking it personally.

The emotionally addicted Four takes everything personally. In the maturity to seek the end of suffering, the willingness to not take the emotions personally means the ability to sink into the very root of negative emotion. At the very bottom, under the superficial sadness, anger, and fear, is the deep despair covering a black hole. By surrendering into the black hole, one can pass through to the other side. Beyond the black hole is the essential nature that is ultimately searched for through story and emotional attachment. The realization of one's true nature leads to a natural state of equanimity that cannot be practiced or imitated. This true state of equanimity allows for the clarity to penetrate ever deeper into the exploration of True Self.

• • •

Point Six

For point Six the holy path is called *courage*. The Six fixation is afraid of fear and believes that courage is the absence of fear. Courage is not this at all. True courage is the willingness to stay true even if fear is experienced. Then fear is not a problem.

Fear is only a problem if it means something. If decisions are made based on fear, then fear is the ruler. If fear does not affect the choices made, then fear is experienced for what it is, without doubt or blame. In the clean experience of fear, fear is discovered to be pure energy that has been identified with the preservation of a "someone."

True courage is to be terrified and to still surrender into the unknown depths of your heart. This is the secret of a silent mind.

• • •

Point Seven

Sobriety is the holy path for the Seven fixation. Sobriety is the willingness to give up the hunger of mind for the new and the different. True sobriety closes the door on any ideas of the future. When this escape hatch of the future is closed, then all the pain and fear that have been avoided by the Seven's constant rush forward will catch up with him.

In the willingness to bear it all, the resulting sobriety is the beginning of true wisdom. One's true nature as wisdom shines forth quite naturally when the waves of desire stop rippling and distorting the surface of mind. This is the doorway into the depths of realization and bliss.

• • •

Point Five

For point Five the holy path is *non-attachment*. Externally, Fives can seem non-attached because of their style of withdrawal. But the withdrawal and hermit-like behavior of the Five are symptoms of deep attachment. There is an attachment to privacy and protection, and the fear of emotional invasion. Attachment happens on both sides of the egoic polarity of fear and desire. Aversion is the attachment motivated by fear, while pursuit is the flip side of chasing desire. All fixations have to face this primal duality and be willing to end it. The Buddha's Noble Truth states: "An end to desire leads to an end to suffering."

For the Five fixation, chasing desirable objects and running from frightening encounters are all surface attachments, compared to the deep attachment to interiorized objects of pleasure. The Five is deeply attached to the mind and its ideas and fantasies.

True non-attachment is the willingness to renounce the mind and its thoughts. This surrender of the precious internal process leads to a deeper realization of the truth of oneself. From that realization, behavior can then be free and unattached to any outcome. Once the desire for any particular outcome is gone, then true non-attachment lets things take their own course quite naturally.

Qualities of Essence

Ananda: The omniscient Lord Buddha, embodiment of universal en-
lightenment, does not single out for praise the Perfection of Generosity,
the Perfection of Goodness, the Perfection of Patience, the Perfection
of Commitment, or the Perfection of Meditation. Only the peerless
Perfection of Wisdom, transcendent insight into the insubstantiality
and transparent functioning of all possible phenomena, does Lord
Buddha continuously mention, ecstatically praise, intensively teach,
and radiantly transmit.

Lord Buddha: You have observed accurately, beloved Ananda. The Per-
fection of Wisdom alone generates and sustains the other five transcen-
dent Perfections that constitute the way of the bodhisattva, the transla-
tion into selflessness of the conventional, egocentric universe.

Prajnaparamita Sutra

Mother of the Buddha's, (Quest Books) Lex Hixon

Fixation is the functioning of selfishness because it is based on
survival. Trying to "work on essence" becomes another act of
selfishness because it strengthens the egoic idea of someone doing
something. When the fixation is not running, essence is shining.
In the moment of selflessness, the veiling of essence is removed.

Regardless, essence is always shining, just as the sun is always
shining. But if you put a finger in your eye, as small and as insig-
nificant as a finger is in relation to the sun, that tiny finger will
blot out the sun and cast you into darkness. You may believe that
the sun is no longer shining, just as you do not notice your funda-

mental essence. It is always even more present than the sun, closer than your breath.

Each fixation is masking a particular quality of essence. When a soul is completely unveiled and shining, the radiance of the light is refracted through each facet of the nine sides of the Enneagram. This shining then assumes different qualities and flavors. As was previously mentioned, the Sufis also gave colors to these denser qualities of essence.

One cannot work to make the soul shine or to accumulate essence. In the willingness to die to selfishness, the transcendent wisdom of the non-reality of the apparent universe reveals itself. In staying true to this revelation, essence naturally shines. The nine essential qualities of a fully shining soul follow.

On this diagram you see that True Self, points 9, 6 and 3, has no color. The character that reflects True Self has a colored Latifa that corresponds to it.

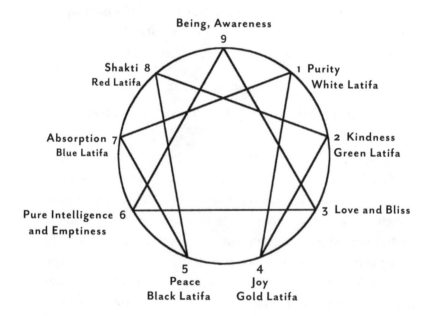

Essence of Body Fixations

Point Nine is the place of immortal being. Nine has two legs, one in Six and one in Three. Since the essence of life, represented by Nine, Six, and Three, is the light that informs and transcends the soul, it does not take on the coloration of the soul's refracted qualities. Pure essence is immortal, intelligent love, the fabric of existence and the source of all. It gives rise to soul, universe, and God, and is transcendent of its own manifestation. It is the shining that animates all denser qualities of essence.

Immortal being at point Nine is flanked by two qualities of being: power (or shakti), the essential quality of point Eight, expressed by the red latifa, and purity, the essential quality of point One, expressed by the white latifa.

Essence of the Emotional Fixations

Love, as the nature of reality, is the essential quality veiled at point Three and is so fundamental it has no color or form. Kindness (called the green latifa by the Sufis) and joy (the gold latifa) are two qualities of love that appear at points Two and Four, respectively.

Essence of the Mental Fixations

The emptiness of point Six is truly empty of everything, even the name emptiness. Absorption (blue latifa) and peace (black latifa) are also qualities of emptiness at points Seven and Five, respectively. The experience of peace has been described as thick, black velvet, still having a subtle quality of existence.

Essence of the Soul

Essence of the subtle body, or soul, gets developed over lifetimes of tests. Whether or not one is self-realized, the soul's essence may be obvious and shining. True character is a reflection of refined essence of being. For the Greeks the possibility of living a happy life is tied to being a Virtuous Character. Virtue cannot be worked or directed but appears after testing as the cross is burned away and the character is left shining.

Character fixation, on the other hand, is a veiling of pure essence, an imitation of essence, and the vehicle for the testing and development of the soul. Each fixation is an imitation of a different quality of essence. Thus, the giving of the Two is an imitation of the essence of kindness. The essential purity of point One is veiled through the angry attachment to finding impurity.

In this way the character fixation is the testing ground to develop true character. To live a truly happy and fulfilled life has two requirements. You must have direct realization of your true nature and the character to live life fully while living in the middle way.

The Guest is inside you!

The Black Hole: Bliss and Despair

A Secret Gateway to Liberation

You know the sprout is hidden in the seed.
We are all struggling, but how far have we gone?
Lose your arrogance now and drop deep within.

– Kabir

The emotional body is one of the three apparent bodies of manifestation. It is an ocean of feelings and latent tendencies. This means that all the emotional waves of all past lives are roiling beneath the surface in this emotional sea. The waves are made up of levels of unexperienced emotion. It is possible to sink into that ocean to discover the layers that have been avoided, and to find what underlies all limited layers and waves. These are the treacherous waters that must be faced in the plunge within. To cross the ocean of samsara is to sink beneath all waves of desire and fear. The final destination, thought to be the far shore, is actually the very bottom of the ocean.

When the karmic momentum of a wave meets the proper conditions on the apparent "outside," the wave surfaces to swamp the conscious mind and to act in ways that appear to be out of control. What gives the waves their force is that they have yet to be directly faced and experienced. Until directly examined, there will be an attachment to the reality of the waves, both as internal experience and external circumstances. These subconscious waves of fixation run the life. The idea of free will is just another thought to justify continuing to play in the waves, thus making waves for the future.

Dropping deep within requires the willingness to experience all that you believe separates you from the truth of yourself as empty, conscious love. In this plunge within, it is possible to bypass all the layers of dormant, subconscious, latent material. However, the dormant layers will still be there to be experienced on your way back into the world. If, by the grace of love, you never resurface from the depths of yourself, then all of these latent tendencies will appear to be experienced and burned in the holy fire of enlightened mind. If egoic identification does resurface, the opportunity will be the same, which is to not move, as everything latent arises to be experienced and burned.

Despair

As in a well of deep water,
dive deeply with clarity.
With speech, mind, and breath stopped,
you will discover the real source of the ego-self.

– Ramana Maharshi Sat Darshan Bashya

At its root, every ego has unexperienced despair. This emotion is at the very bottom of the well. Despair is the recognition of the hopeless futility of the situation. It is based on the recognition of mortality and the inevitability of death. Ironically, death is the gatekeeper at the threshold to immortality.

While despair is at the root of every ego, it is rarely fully experienced. It is believed to be simply too painful to bear. In order to avoid the experience of despair, the ego is buffered by more superficial emotions. In our time, when someone comes close to despair, it is called depression, and treated with drugs in order to avoid directly experiencing it.

Most people live their lives on the very surface of things. This is the "ignorance is bliss" school of thought. On the most superficial level, it is easy to see that the petty hurts, frustrations, irritations, nervousness, and other emotions are generated by a circumstantial story that is being taken personally. Combined with the internal and external dialogue that generates moods and feelings, people are forever feeling blamed, placing blame, or feeling hurt in an endless cycle of personal story. Below this superficial level are un-examined emotions that generate the story as a buffer against the actual experience of being fully present in whatever is arising.

Under the mental waves of the personal story is found the layering of emotion. The order of the layering is common to most fixations, though the Nine fixation usually has a different order from the others. For the Nine, the emotion of rage is down near the bottom with despair. Rage for the Nine fixation is believed to be a hopeless expression of impotence in the face of the catastrophe of life. When the Nine fixation is willing to experience the homicidal rage that is at the bottom, this is very close to the core despair.

Above the rage for the Nine is fear; it is much easier for a Nine to feel fear than rage. But fear is also unpleasant and so above fear is hurt and sadness. It is much easier for a Nine to feel sad and a little depressed than to drop all the way in to the deeper feelings. Even sadness gets buffered by the more superficial, artificially generated emotions of the personal story.

It is easier to feel frustrated, misunderstood, or confused rather than to feel what is deeper. Often when dropping in to experience the deeper emotions, the Nine will reach a place of numbness or deadness and not proceed any further. This is the defense mechanism of self-narcotization, defending against a painful experience.

• • •

The other fixations are layered in a slightly different order. For most, fear is the emotion covering despair. On top of fear is sadness, and above sadness is anger. But there are always exceptions to this. Certain fear points suppress anger, which is too dangerous to express, under sadness and hurt.

It is always possible to drop from the surface directly into the depths. However, if there are layers of unexperienced emotion that have been skipped over or denied, these layers will reappear later to be experienced.

The Black Hole

On a very practical level, it is possible to start at the very surface, and by directly experiencing the surface emotion, to then fall deeper to the underlying emotion. For example, if you are angry with someone and are willing to feel the anger fully without suppressing it and without discharging it, under the anger you will often find hurt. If you experience the hurt, under that you may find fear. If you then fully experience the fear and drop beneath it, you will find despair. If you are willing to drop all the way into despair, you will eventually fall through into a "black hole."

One of the many gifts of the Enneagram is that by examining the structure of the nine fixations, we can discover that at the root of every ego, there is a veiling of a black hole. All fixation is an attempt to keep from falling into the emptiness of the black hole. Points Four and Five, at the bottom of the Enneagram, are the two fixations that are most acutely aware of the existence of the black hole. The Four avoids the black hole by clinging to emotion, and the Five deals with the terror of falling into the black hole by attachment to mental ideas.

Certain properties being proposed for black holes discovered in outer space are remarkably similar to the black holes discovered in inner space. When one plunges within, descending into a black hole of nothingness, there is a collapsing of the event horizon. Scientists describe this collapse in outer space by saying that light waves cannot escape the pull of the black hole, and thus the past and the future are sucked into the hole. The collapsing of the event horizon in inner space is the dissolution of a personal past and future, along with the story of a personal me.

The black hole is an escape hatch out of the limited emotional body into limitless essence. Diving into the black hole reveals the possibility of the direct realization of essence, ending all identification with the ego. However, if there is an attempt to turn this insight into a technique to gain something, or to not feel negative emotions, the medicine is turned to poison, and fixation continues to run the life.

• • •

Example of Falling In

The following dialogue is a clear example of using emotional experience as a vehicle for self-inquiry. The following session took place at Esalen Institute in Big Sur, California. The participant has an Eight fixation.

Participant: I am really pissed off! I can't believe that she did that to me.

Eli: This is a very familiar feeling isn't it?

P: Yes.

E: Would you like to try an experiment to discover what is deeper? You might be surprised.

P: Okay. Anything would be better than this.

E: You say you are really pissed off. Now feel that fully, without any story attached, and what is the pure emotion?

P: I am really angry.

E: Yes, that's right. You are really angry. (*Anger is now the emotion that was underlying the "story" of "pissed off."*) Feel the anger fully without a story. And now, what is under the anger?

P: I feel sad. I am hurt that she would betray me like that. (*At this point, there is still a story of blame for what is being experienced.*)

E: Yes, you feel sad. Feel the sadness fully, without a story or meaning. And what is even deeper?

P: I am afraid I will lose her. I am afraid it will be like all the other relationships I've lost.

E: Yes, you are afraid. Invite all the fear of this lifetime to be experienced now. And what is even deeper under the fear?

P: It's the pits. It's some kind of hell. I feel like I'm never gonna get it. I feel like it's never going to get better.

E: That's right. You feel like it's never going to get better. Feel that emotion fully without the story. Feel the pure despair of it.

P: It feels endless.

E: Yes, it feels endless. Let yourself drown in it now. Fall in so deeply that there is no coming out. (*Long pause.*) When you fall all the way in, what is even deeper?

P: It's like I'm falling through space. I'm falling into a well of blackness.

E: Yes, that's right, you are falling into a well of blackness, a well with no sides. Fall all the way in, and when you come out the bottom, let me know what you are experiencing.

P: It's empty everywhere, but it's a full empty. There is love everywhere.

E: Yes, love everywhere. Are you separate from this love?

P: No.

E: Then who are you?

P: I am the love.

E: Yes, it's true, you are love.

• • •

Practical Application

At every moment, you have the opportunity to stop and fully experience everything that is here. If you are willing, you can experience all the layers of mind and emotion, all the way down to the core and through to emptiness. It takes no special space or preparation, only the willingness to face everything. It is only through this facing that you can discover the total insubstantiality of all waves of identity.

Before meeting my teacher many years ago, I was in Germany leading a retreat in which I was just developing a working model of black holes. My German assistant was driving us for the early morning sitting meditation. After we were in the car for a few minutes, she told me that we might run out of gas and not make it to the sitting.

My first impulse was anger at her carelessness. I needed to be there before anyone else so that I was sitting when they all came in. I thought I was serving as a role model, and now she was ruining it with her forgetfulness.

Normally, I would have verbally attacked her, as I had done for most of my life. I would have discharged my anger by projecting it onto her and blaming her for both our situation and my anger. Or possibly at another point in time, after I had done some work on myself, instead of shouting at her I might have tried repressing the anger, but it still would have come out as a sarcastic cutting comment to let her know she was wrong.

This time, I just experienced the situation. Under the anger, I found the hurt that she had let me down. Under the hurt, I was shocked to discover pride. What I had called "being in service" was actually running on pride. I had no idea! I felt the spiritual pride completely and then the burning humiliation of that. Under the humiliation, I dropped into deep, joyful bliss. All the while, my driver was driving along unaware of what was going on next to her, except that when I sunk into the experience of bliss, the quality of the energy in the car changed. She stopped worrying about the gas and the tone of her voice changed. We sat in silence together as we drove up to the retreat center in plenty of time and with just enough gas. If we had run out of gas, it would still have been a perfect teaching. It was not about changing the outcome, but rather, the willingness to give up all attachment to personal outcome or to being right. Through this kind of willingness, one can discover that the whole universe is medicine.

The experience of dropping beneath the surface breaks the trance of the fixation's story of reality. What seems to be real on the surface is realized to be a shallow version of reality. Dropping in beneath the surface gives a direct experience of essence. If the drop is pure and deep, you fall into the bliss of true Self.

Bliss

I speak about Sahaja Samadhi, where you remain calm, composed, and still, even while the body is active. You realize that you are moved by the deeper, real Self within. You have no worries, no anxieties, no cares. You realize that nothing belongs to you, and everything is done by Something with which you are in conscious union. The mind is free from doubt and choosing. It is sure of the truth. It feels the presence of the real. Even when it is active, it knows that it is active in the Reality, the Self, the Supreme Being.

– Ramana Maharshi Sat Darshan Bhashya

Levels of Samadhi

In Sanskrit, absorption in bliss is called *samadhi*. There are many different types of samadhi catalogued in the Hindu cosmology. Most samadhi is the plunge within to the bliss of the Self. In the process of waking up to one's true nature, the experience of bliss is as essential as the experience of despair.

As was just displayed, dropping through the black hole is a limited form of samadhi. It is an experience that has a duration and an end. This is called "throwing the bucket into the well with the rope still attached." The rope is the mind. At the end of the experience, the mind resurfaces as an ego-identified someone who just had an experience.

There is a well-known story that illustrates this form of samadhi:

Once a king sent out word to his kingdom that he would give a horse to anyone in his kingdom who could remain in samadhi for one month. A yogi in the hills heard the news. He had always wanted a horse, and he knew he could do it. He presented himself at the court. The yogi went into deep samadhi and never moved. One month passed, and he still didn't move. Six months passed, and then a year. Years started to roll by. Soon the king was dead, and his son was on the throne. One day the yogi opened his eyes, looked around, and said, "Where's my horse?"

The value of this kind of samadhi is that you are immersed in the bliss of yourself. The downside is that it is a limited experience, which has a beginning and an end. As long as the fixated mind believes itself to be real, the *idea* of yourself remains the unexamined apparent ground of being. Breakthroughs, states of samadhi and bliss, appear like holes in the ground of personal being. Once the experience is over, the reconstituted *I* then claims the experience as its own. The egoic *I* searches for more and more spiritual experience in the hopes that the experience will become permanent, and *I* will become enlightened. Yet all experience is limited, and enlightenment is merely the permanent absence of a belief in a limited "I."

The next level of samadhi is throwing the bucket into the well without a rope. This is the willingness to end all identification with an individual *I* who is having a spiritual experience. The personal entity is seen to be non-existent, and the individual life is then lived as emptiness and love.

The last level of samadhi, Sahaja Samadhi, is not a plunge within at all but a natural resting in yourself as yourself. Regardless of the experience, whether blissful or painful, regardless of circumstance, whether positive or negative, turning away from the truth of yourself never occurs. This is called Self-realization.

The Way of Silence

If you want to be free, get to know your real self. It has no form, no appearance, no root, no basis, no abode, but is lively and buoyant. It responds with versatile facility, but its function cannot be located. Therefore when you look for it, you become further from it; when you seek it you turn away from it all the more.

– Zen Teaching

We have seen how the Enneagram gives us a reflective surface for exposing the artifices of mind. Pollution, or the fluctuating mind, is generated by the character fixation. Grasping, rejecting, subjective judgments, and artificiality are the hallmarks of fixation. Character fixation is a crystallization of the mind-stuff of eons of desire waves, or fluctuations. This crystallization is experienced as "me and my past and my future." The waves are the thoughts of "what I fear" and "what I want." All of this is the running of fixation.

Once the subtle structures of mind activity are realized, one can stop making waves, and the mind can surrender and come to rest. To surrender is to give up making waves or fluctuations in the mind-stuff. The result of this surrender is peace, which is not numbness or blankness or even calmness, but deep, true, essential peace and love. Peace is realized as blissful stillness. Love is experienced as immortal being, conscious of itself.

• • •

When most of us speak of self today, we are most likely referring to the physical body with its attendant thoughts and emotions. Yet, it is the belief that all the fluctuations of body, mind, and emotion are my true self that block the clear perception of the true Self. Clear perception is only possible when there is no pollution. When there is no pollution, the mind is silent. This silent mind is the goal of all spiritual practice. It is both the path to realization and its fruit.

The great dilemma, then, is how to silence the mind, thus ending mind pollution and directly realizing the truth of oneself as pure, undifferentiated consciousness. Many have tasted the sublime sweetness of true silence. I am not referring to relative quiet as opposed to noise, but the transcendent roar of silence that gives birth to, and supports all, relative quiet and relative noise.

• • •

This realization that comes with a silent mind has been in our gene pool for quite some time in many traditions around the world

St. John of the Cross, living in the middle ages in Spain, expressed the profound realization of a silent mind quite beautifully when he wrote:

I entered into unknowing, and there I remained unknowing, transcending all knowledge. That perfect knowledge was of peace and holiness and held at no remove. In profound solitude, it was something so secret that I was left stammering, transcending all knowledge.

Many people in our time and culture have had a taste of the truth beyond all knowledge and all form. Whether through meditation, near-death experiences, psychedelics, or watching a sunset, many have experienced the descent of grace and tasted the sacredness, the stillness, and the purity that is at the core of all. The question remains, how does one make this often-fleeting glimpse the permanent condition, undistorted by the pollution of fluctuation?

Many practices for relatively quieting the mind have been tried with varying degrees of success. For most, the final cut has remained elusive at best.

The secret of a silent mind is non-action. This usually gets heard by the mind as a "doing" not-doing, and it is not that. Pure non-action is free from fixation and identity. It is selfless and reveals the true non-ground of emptiness. Free-falling into the unknown never ends. This is the secret of non-action.

It was not until I had passed through many spiritual traditions, meeting many gurus and saints, that I finally came across the pure transmission of this immaculate realization. In the vast universe of spirituality, where claims and counterclaims, cover-ups and frauds run rife, there is one who is universally respected as a true, Self-realized one who did no harm. His devotees called him Ramana Maharshi.

Ramana's suggested method of cutting the knot of egoic mind is called self-inquiry. Self- inquiry can best be characterized as the silent mind discovering its source.

Traditionally, self-inquiry is described as a process of the mind turning within to discover: Who am I? Am I this body? Am I these thoughts? Am I these feelings? As the silent mind notices the arising of the *I* thought, it follows this thought to its source where it dissolves and the true *I* shines forth.

A silent mind is a mind free of entanglements. A silent mind has given up the struggle to be right, to know, to do, and to have. In the deepest realization of truth, all entanglements and struggles are burned in recognition of their non-reality.

In the Buddhist and Hindu traditions, the transmission of a silent mind is passed from the Realized One to the mature seeker. For this, a true teacher is necessary. This teacher who can transmit a silent mind by the radiance of being in Sanskrit is called a Sat-Guru. Guru being teacher and Sat meaning Immortal Being.

· · ·

When I first began my spiritual search in 1971 at the age of twenty-four, one of the first books I read was Lao Tzu's *Tao Teh Ching*. I read the description of a silent mind, but I did not know how to get there from here. I could not imagine what that would be like or what my life would look like if I could achieve this exalted state. With the use of psychedelics, I experienced the bliss of a silent mind. But the experience would never last, as it seemed I had no control over the process of thinking. For eighteen years, I searched through the various spiritual traditions but never found a final answer.

On January 19, 1990, I wandered into the home of a yet unknown teacher in Lucknow, India. Sitting with him on his bed, I found the end of my spiritual path. In the instant that we met, I knew that this was the one I had been searching for all my life. I knew that I was sitting with, and facing, my own Self.

Although not needed, a confirming sign were the two items on the wall of his tiny room. One was a larger-than-life photograph of his teacher, Ramana Maharshi. The other was a Sri Yantra. If you don't know what this looks like, check my website. The Sri Yantra had been my sacred symbol and the mark of my organization for over a decade before our meeting. But these confirming signs were secondary to the meeting itself.

As soon as I saw him, I fell in love. We looked in each other's eyes, and I felt overwhelmed with bliss. He asked me, "Why have you come?"

"I am ready to wake up," I replied. He laughed and hugged me and I knew I was home.

After three days I said, "Papaji, I have been with you three days now, and I'm still not enlightened."

He said, "Yes, I am surprised, a smart boy like you."

"What should I do?" I asked.

"Let me tell you what my teacher told me. Let the mind be still. Do not give rise to a thought."

"How do I do that?"

"Your mind is silent now, isn't it?"

I had to say that in his presence there was an overwhelming sense of bliss and a deep silence of mind. "Yes, it is," I replied.

He said, "Now look down into the emptiness and watch for the next thought."

I did. I watched the next thought start to rise like a bubble slowly taking form. I did not touch it. Instead, it sank back into emptiness.

He smiled and said, "Vigilance is not following the next thought. You are now on a razor's edge. When on a razor's edge, don't carry a load. Even one thought is too much of a load."

I followed his instructions, and for the next month the silence deepened to become a deafening roar. Living free of thought, life continued rolling of its own momentum. Empty consciousness observed it all in bliss.

My teacher asked that I take this realization back to the world and to the work I was doing before we met. This book is part of my expression of his wishes.

• • •

I find now, almost thirty years since meeting Papaji, that more and more people are discovering the secret of a silent mind. In the near past, it was considered impossible. Now it has entered as a meme into our gene pool. Being *woke* is a new cultural idiom that expresses the possibility for everyone to stop the mind and wake up.

Stopping the mind is not about effort. It is not about one thought dueling with all other thoughts. It is merely using the Enneagram to see your identification with a personal story that is really not "unique" or "personal" at all, and to discover the willingness to end it.

What ends is not the mind, but a certain function of mind. Mind that is focused on a personal identity runs laterally from the past to the future, and back. When this running of mind ceases, the mind naturally plunges within. In the plunge within to the source of itself, the mind is now the vehicle for the revelation of the depths. This change is merely from a horizontal route to a vertical route. The mind stops running backward and forward and instead sinks in and comes up. In this sinking within, the mind is realized to be nothing other than pure consciousness, the true Self, who one really is.

This is not the end but the beginning. All that led up to this moment is pre-history. All that follows contributes to the soul's deepening realization as it merges in final union with the divine.

Later, we will be tested by the temptations to fall back into conditioned existence. When we stand in integrity in the face of temptations, fears and doubts, we deepen into being a virtuous human being. We live a life fully incarnate in the deep pleasure of being alive and serve as a beacon of possibility for those we encounter along the way.

• • •

May all beings be happy and free.

• • •

About the Leela Foundation

Eli founded and teaches through The Leela Foundation, a non-profit organization supporting world peace and freedom through universal Self-realization.

For more information about the Leela Foundation, please visit www.leela.org. On Facebook visit both: Leela Community and The Leela School of Awakening. And on YouTube our channels are The Leela Foundation and The Leela School of Awakening.

At the First International Enneagram Conference at Stanford University in 1992, Eli Jaxon-Bear presented a radically new model of the structure of the soul and psyche based on The Enneagram of Liberation. By joining self-inquiry with his map of ego fixation, he has presented a model for universal self-realization. Linking this teaching with Pythagorus, he found the mystery school that he was searching for for over forty years.

In 2005 he founded the Leela School of Awakening operating in Sydney, Australia, Amsterdam, the Netherlands and Ashland, Oregon in the US.

He continues to lead retreats around the world..

He has been living with his partner and wife since 1976. They currently reside in Ashland, Oregon.

Eli meets people and teaches through the Leela Foundation, www.leela.org, and The Leela School of Awakening, www.leelaschool.org

CPSIA information can be obtained
at www.ICGtesting.com
Printed in the USA
FSHW011259290621
82797FS